THE OTHER
SIDE
OF DIVORCE

Other Books by Helen Kooiman Hosier

FORGIVENESS IN ACTION
GOING SIDEWAYS (*with Duane Pederson*)
DAY OF MIRACLES (*with Duane Pederson*)
JOYFULLY EXPECTANT: MEDITATIONS BEFORE BABY COMES
PLEASE PRAY FOR THE CABBAGES: PINT-SIZE PARABLES
   FOR GROWNUPS
CAMEOS: WOMEN FASHIONED BY GOD
SMALL TALK
LIVING WORDS OF COMFORT AND CHEER
TRANSFORMED: BEHIND THE SCENES WITH BILLY GRAHAM
SILHOUETTES: WOMEN BEHIND GREAT MEN
WALTER KNOTT: KEEPER OF THE FLAME

THE OTHER SIDE OF DIVORCE

Helen Kooiman Hosier

HAWTHORN BOOKS, INC.
W. Clement Stone, Publisher
New York

THE OTHER SIDE OF DIVORCE

Library of Congress Catalog Card Number: 74-15642

ISBN: 0-8015-5644-9

1 2 3 4 5 6 7 8 9 10

Contents

	Foreword	vii
	Acknowledgments	ix
	Introduction	1
1	Defining the Problem	5
2	Superwoman or SuperGod?	11
3	The Search	16
4	The Whole Counsel of God	25
5	Peace	33
6	"Never Get a Divorce!"	41
7	Jesus and a Divorcée	48
8	What about the Church and Divorce?	55
9	What about the Children of Divorce?	74
10	Remorse? Or Triumph?	99
11	The New Dimension	107
12	Remarriage a No-No?	116
13	Are There Any Deterrents to Divorce?	136
14	Togetherness	151
15	The Happily Married Do Communicate	165
16	First Corinthians 13: Agape Love	177
17	Divorce Is . . .	186
18	Is Divorce Unpardonable?	191
	Bibliographical Notes	195

Dedicated to healing and helping hurting hearts

"Let all who are discouraged take heart. Let us praise the Lord together, and exalt his name. For I cried to him and he answered me! He freed me from all my fears. Others too were radiant at what he did for them. . . . Oh, put God to the test and see how kind he is! See for yourself the way his mercies shower down on all who trust in him. . . . The Lord is close to those whose hearts are breaking; he rescues those who are humbly sorry for their sins. . . . Great is the Lord who enjoys helping his child! . . . . Lord, You have listened to my troubles and have seen the crisis in my soul."

Selected portions from favorite
psalms from *The Living Bible*

Foreword

Marriage is the most intimate and the most lasting of all human relationships. It therefore can be plagued with problems of every variety. The Holy Scriptures do not begin to tell us all these problems and their answers. We are left to Christian conscience and common sense to thread our way through them.

Because American evangelicals have kept to a very simplified view of marriage and divorce on the surface they have created a "divorce underground": Great numbers of evangelical lay people and ministers, who have been divorced on the quiet, have remarried, and carry on as though nothing has happened. This is stark unrealism.

Helen Hosier has dared to unmask this unrealistic view of marriage and divorce. It is time that the issue is faced for what it is and not piously glossed over.

The only way this could be done with any effectiveness was for a devoted evangelical who had gone through the divorce procedure to write about it. An outsider would not know the dynamics of the evangelical community.

Helen tells us her story. We can live along with her in her problems. We can see what the down-to-earth issues are. She relates her experience to biblical texts and to the view of the church towards divorce so that her appeal is not a pure appeal to experience.

The message of her book is to be helpful and healing. I hear about once every two weeks of some Christian friend, some evangelical minister, and yes, even some evangelical missionaries who go through the divorce procedure. I wonder how many of them suffer needlessly from feelings of guilt and shame based on an oversimplified, unrealistic ethic. Helen Hosier's book could have been a great help to them. I trust it will be of help to those whose marriages—contrary to their expectations to maintain them in this life until death—are coming apart; who want help, guidance, and advice from someone in the evangelical community who has gone through it. And, having gone through it, writes about it with discernment, compassion, wisdom, and loyalty to evangelical doctrine.

BERNARD RAMM
Eastern Baptist Theological Seminary
Philadelphia, Pennsylvania

Acknowledgments

In no way does this book represent the thinking of one person. Rather, it is a distillation gleaned from the minds and hearts of many individuals, material I have been gathering for some time, both from personal encounters and interviews and from a vast number of books and articles, as well as newspaper clippings and sermons preached.

In particular, I am deeply grateful to those who honestly and willingly opened up their innermost feelings—even though it meant the reopening of wounds—and who unveiled their hearts. Those who had experienced the trauma that accompanies divorce showed great empathy and a deep desire to share with the hope that in so doing others could be spared the hurt and heartache they had endured. Over and over I heard, "It hurts to say this and to bring up the past but if it will help others and if it will make the Christian world really understand and realize what they are doing to those of us who have been through divorce, then it's worth it. . . . " These people will remain anonymous, though they are not afraid to be identified nor are they ashamed of what they have had to do. I, however, choose to give them anonymity for the sake of their families, themselves, and the new lives that with God's help they are attempting to rebuild.

There were others who read the completed manuscript and suffered through all of this with me. You have been so loving and gracious. You, too, shall remain unnamed, but I am grateful for your discernment and loving concern.

To all who prayed and cared: Thank you. Simple words, but said with depth of feeling.

Introduction

It was in February, 1971, that the judge pounded his gavel in a southern California courtroom, which signified the end had come to a marriage of twenty-two years. It happens every day in courtrooms all over the land, but that day it happened to us. That brief session in the presence of the judge, the lawyers, and others in the courtroom, was not really the end, however. The end of that marriage relationship had occurred many years ago. That particular experience in the lives of those who go through a divorce is one of agony, heartbreak, inner turmoil, mental anguish, and confusion. There is anger and despair—all the ingredients one would rather not encounter in any kind of situation. The courtroom scene is something one does not like to relive in one's thinking.

But while the incident in the courtroom is unpleasant, so are many of the memories and experiences that contribute to the death of love and the final end of a marriage. This book will not dwell on such painful events—mine or anyone else's. The book is based upon actual interviews, however, with divorced Christian men and women. What I relate to you is fact, not fiction.

Some time after my divorce was final, I received a long-distance phone call. The call took me by surprise. It was from someone whom I greatly admired and respected in the Christian world. The caller suggested I consider going back into my marriage and added that because I was a writer I might then write a book relating my experience. "Think how many people could be blessed and helped by such a book," was his comment. "Many marriages might be salvaged, many broken homes put back together . . . "

I was grateful for that call and such concern. It was a genuine expression of Christian love. I still hold that person in great respect with high esteem. But that kind of book from me has not been written. However, almost from the start the present book became a burden on my heart. I was experiencing what happens on the other side of divorce, and I knew no one could possibly understand this unless they had been there. I knew of no book that had been written, directed specifically to Christians, from a divorced Christian, attempting to help and to heal and to bring some understanding and a measure of hope to divorced people themselves, their children, and others touched by divorce.

There is a breach in the Christian world caused by divorce. In some instances it is a chasm of immense proportions. I long to see this breach mended; I long to erect some kind of a bridge for mutual understanding and acceptance.

While this book needed to be written, and I deeply sensed this, still I didn't want to be the one to do it. I argued with myself and shoved the thought aside. But the thought continued to surface. Why didn't I want to be the one to write such a book? The question deserved a reply. I faced it honestly: (1) I didn't want to hurt my former husband, his family, and our children; (2) I didn't want to write anything that would encourage divorce or provide a convenient "out" or "escape" to those contemplating divorce; (3) I didn't want to say anything that might be misconstrued as being vindictive, or that would be misinterpreted as bitterness; (4) I didn't want to be accused of being defensive; and last but not least, (5) I didn't want to bring reproach upon Christianity and the name of Christ.

In the final analysis, as I looked at these reasons I had to admit that God could take care of every one. He knew my heart; he knew my love for him and others in the body of

Christ; could I not trust him to help me say what needed to be said in a spirit of love? The burden remained until finally the needed effort was put forth. What you will read is the result of much prayer being made by many loving, concerned Christians who were aware of this undertaking.

There were some friends who tried to dissuade me from writing the book. I do respect and value their judgment and opinions also. Some of these same individuals have expressed the belief that this book and remarriage will be, in their words, "career suicide." These, too, are loving, concerned Christians.

I must state, however, what has become impressed upon my thinking. I do so in the same spirit of love with which the rest of this book is written. I question the use of the words "career suicide" and ask if "career murder" would not be more accurate. Who is killing what? Does God close doors of opportunity for those who speak the truth in love for him? I dare to believe that God is still seeking men and women who will stand in the gap and strive to rebuild walls for him (see Ezek. 22:30).

> Blessed is the man who trusts in
> the Lord and has made the Lord
> his hope and confidence. The heart
> is the most deceitful thing there
> is, and desperately wicked. No one
> can really know how bad it is! Only
> the Lord knows! *He searches all*
> *hearts and examines deepest motives*
> so he can give to each person his
> right reward according to his deeds—
> how he has lived (Jer. 17:7, 9, 10).
> [Author's italics]

God has repeatedly told us throughout the Word that he and he only can see into the heart to search and examine motives. He reserves that right for himself. As I search the

Scriptures, I can find no place where God today wants his people to prophesy doom for each other based on limited knowledge (referring to those who comprise the body of Christ). Paul urges us to seek the gift of prophecy (1 Cor. 14:1), but he tells us, "Let love be your greatest aim" (vs. 1).

I thank God for the gift of writing that he has given to me, but I hasten to say that it has never been my desire to be a career writer. I have simply used what he has given to me in an effort to bring glory to him. And so this book is a heartfelt plea for love and understanding between the divorced individual and those who have not experienced divorce. My plea is this: In the name of our merciful Lord, don't slam shut the doors of the church, the doors of our Christian colleges and businesses, and the doors of your hearts and leave the divorced person to face the tomorrows alone. God is still with that one who is divorced; but the companionship and fellowship of Christian friends is also needed.

1
Defining the Problem

God hates divorce (Mal. 2:16),* and so do I!

And so do those Christians who have been divorced!

When someone comes to me asking about divorce, my first words to them are, "Don't. Don't divorce if there is any spark of love left for your mate at all. Rebuild on that love; work to rekindle that love into a real flame. It can be done. Many books and magazine articles have been and are being written to show that people on the verge of divorce have successfully put their marriages back together, better and stronger than they ever were to begin with."

There are many marriages, however, that are sub-ideal, in which the partners are living in what I refer to throughout this book as a state of undivorce, yet striving to keep the marriage together while living in great unpeace and disharmony. The people about whom I write have come out of situations like that. There is another side to divorce that is seldom discussed. The banging of a judge's gavel, while it signifies the end of a relationship, may also be the beginning of a whole new life of beautiful fruitful living for the Lord,

*All scripture quotations, unless otherwise noted, are from *The Living Bible*. Other versions of the Bible quoted are the *Authorized* (*King James*) *Version* (*AV*), the *New American Standard* (*NAS*), *Phillips New Testament in Modern English* (*PT*), and *The Amplified Bible* (*AB*).

the people involved, and others with whom they live and have contact. Divorce, while it is painful and tragic, can lead to the ultimate rebirth of an individual, a new relationship with Christ, a closer walk, leaning on him for direction and support, a rediscovery of meaning in living and personal growth.

When efforts toward reconciliation and working out the problems fail, when professional counsel has been sought, when pastoral counsel has been given, when prayers have been made, and still marital discord prevails, do those on the outside of a situation have the right to stand in judgment and say that such individuals have no right to divorce?

For too long the Christian world has backed off from the complex issues of divorce. No longer, however, can they be ignored. While it is true according to surveys that the "old-time religion" adherents have the lowest incidence of divorce, still divorce is touching Christian homes as well. What is being done for divorced Christians by other Christians who are not divorced? What is your church doing? Are efforts made to redeem them, to open up doors of hope and opportunity for them? Or are they being forced to plunge into deeper despair? These questions are being asked by many theologians and others who are greatly concerned and who observe the inflation rate of divorces; and the same questions are being raised by divorced individuals themselves, many of whom experience nothing but rejection and feel shunned and scorned.

"I don't like being made to feel that I am a second-class citizen of the Christian world," said a middle-aged divorcee. Her sentiments were voiced by others. "I've been denied positions of responsibility and leadership," said another, with a hurt tone in his voice.

Still another commented, "I have so much I'd like to share from my deep-water experience . . ."

It is an established fact—both biblical and in the lives of

countless Christians—that it is the fiery trials, the great tragedies, the times of testing and going through deep waters, the agony and heartbreak that most often produce in us that which enables us to identify with and help others. One needs only to look at the lives of the saints, past and present, to recognize the validity of that statement. My own experience in relating to the hurting hearts of others is so much different now than it ever was before I was divorced. As I speak to groups, I now find myself counseling in ways I was totally unprepared for before. When I hold a dear, sobbing woman in my arms—someone I've never met before—following a sharing time, there is a love passing between us that lay dormant for half of my lifetime. This, I have discovered, is a common experience among divorced individuals. We loved and cared for others before, but there is a different dimension to our capacity to love and forgive now. This is confirmed to us by those who knew us before or may have heard us speak then and now.

Those who take a firm stand against divorce believe they are standing on solid biblical ground. I, too, believe what the Bible has to say about divorce. Permanence in marriage is God's ideal. But those of us who are divorced have access to God's Word also—the whole counsel of God—and we have used it—we are using it—and we have access to God and his power to work on our behalf. We have been and are praying; we have even put out "fleeces" and have experienced definite and dramatic answers to prayer. I can assure you, contrary to what some may think, God is still our comfort. He does not desert his children in their times of trial, even through the trauma of divorce. David the psalmist said, "For thou God wilt light my candle; the Lord my God will enlighten my darkness" (Ps. 18:28, *AV*). "He is a shield for *everyone* who hides behind him" (vs. 30). [Author's italics]

At the outset of my divorce action, I invited a friend to have lunch with me. I loved her very much, admired her, and marveled at the way God used her in touching lives for him. I knew that it would be difficult for her and others to accept what I knew I must do. I said to her, and I repeat it to you, that those of us who are divorced can do without the Christian world's condemnation; we don't need your approval on what we, after long and serious thought, prayer, and work, feel we must do; but we do need justice with love.

The churches' rigidity in regard to divorce and its opposition to remarriage have often resulted in pronouncements from pulpits, articles in magazines, and strong words in books denouncing divorce as sin. This then is reflected in the attitudes of parishioners towards those who do divorce, giving occasion for gossip, criticism, ostracism, and censure of the worst kind. It is as if those who aren't divorced feel they have some kind of license or special right to do this. This is one kind of "sinner," you see, whose guilt and sinfulness is a matter of open public record. Such is the problem that exists, and it is very real and difficult, I recognize, for those on each side of the fence. For it is true that an invisible, but nonetheless real, barrier can exist.

In the eyes of many Christians, there are some who have divorced who may not have "the biblical grounds for divorce." I would entreat you to remember that you do not know all the facts, and God does. God is holy, but he is not unrealistic. There are many of us who simply will not, cannot, reveal all that has gone on in our marriages. We do not wish to inflict this upon others. It is in bad taste, for we do not wish to talk about our former mates in a disparaging way. Is it not far better to leave the matter with God and accept us for what we are—his children, saved by his grace, pardoned and loved by him because of Christ and God's forgiveness?

If God can forgive, why can't his people? Or does the Bible actually say that divorce and remarriage are unforgivable sins? When the Word declares that if we confess our sins, he is faithful and just to forgive us our sins, and to cleanse us from *all* unrighteousness (1 John 1:9), does it mean that or doesn't it? Must divorced people forever after carry a stigma enforced upon them by the Christian world? Must we remain second-class citizens of the Christian community where we would like to continue in fellowship and in work for the Lord?

Is divorce too great an evil for human Christian forgiveness? Are divorced people to be pushed to the sidelines and avoided or ignored? Are they to be denied the right to remarry and establish happy homes? Where is Christian justice for divorced people today? Where do you personally stand in regard to showing love and justice? Have we forgotten what Jesus said? "For if you forgive other people their failures, your Heavenly Father will also forgive you. But if you will not forgive other people, neither will your Heavenly Father forgive you your failure" (Matt. 6:12, 14, 15, *PT*).

Paul, who had much to say about divorce, nevertheless had this to say about forgiveness:

> As, therefore, God's picked representatives of the new humanity, purified and beloved of God himself, be merciful in action, kindly in heart, humble in mind. Accept life, and be most patient and tolerant with one another, always ready to forgive if you have a difference with anyone. Forgive as freely as the Lord has forgiven you. And, above everything else, be truly loving, for love is the golden chain of all the virtues (Col. 3:12–14, *PT*).

Is that forgiveness, or isn't it? *As Christ gives it.* It's costly. Is it meant to include divorced people, or are we told to exclude them?

In an effort to mend the breach caused among Christians

9

by divorce, and with the prayerful hope that this book can provide some kind of bridge for mutual understanding and acceptance, you will be asked to focus upon that which is true, facing the divorce problem realistically. The Apostle Paul has exhorted us to do that very thing:

> Finally, brethen, whatsoever things are true, whatsoever things are honest, whatsoever things are just, whatsoever things are pure, whatsoever things are lovely, whatsoever things are of good report; if there be any virtue, and if there be any praise, *think on these things* (Phil. 4:8, *AV*). [Author's italics]

THINK ON THESE THINGS

God hates divorce (Mal. 2:16); but he loves the sinner.

Touch not mine anointed, and do them no harm (Ps. 105:15).

2
Superwoman or SuperGod?

"You've been through so much. You always manage to bounce back. You'll be all right." My friend was standing by, offering consolation. Her presence was of tremendous help and encouragement. She was loyal and dear. How I loved her! How much I needed her! "I'm not taking sides," she had said at the outset of the divorce action, "I love you both." With her and with some others, I discovered it was not going to be a case of friends: mine, hers, ours? She proved true to her word, and I was glad.

I don't recall my reply, but that day I wasn't bouncing, nor did I have the feeling that I'd ever bounce back again. At best I'm sure my reply was a feeble halfhearted attempt to be funny. Funny, cute, clever—a familiar pattern, with the newly divorced especially. Brave fronts that mask the separation shock, the bleeding insides and emotional wounds; we wear them with an air of self-confidence that we do not feel. It does not seem to matter whether the divorce was a mutual decision or if one party walked out on the other; there is emotional-disentanglement pain for both.

Maybe that day I said something like, "The Lord's been good. He's always faithful." I meant it. I said it often, and deep inside I truly meant it and believed it. But it had become a stock answer. It sounded good and, of course, it was expected of me; but the hurting me knew that I should be saying it with more conviction.

The latest in a long series of hurts had about unglued me. My heart ached. Another cruel blow had been dealt, and my innards felt as if they'd been scrambled. Scrambled? Mangled? Was there anything left? The inner resources that always saw me through now seemed perilously close to being exhausted. I felt drained. Yes, strained to breaking. Someone else described himself as feeling like the walking wounded. Another woman said she felt as if her legs had gone on "automatic," carrying her through empty space. One person commented, "My internal inventory was zero, and I was haunted by feelings of failure and guilt."

What does it feel like to be divorced? Who can explain the paralyzing impact of the sudden aloneness and uncertainty about the future? In the cauldron of our emotions, all sorts of internal feelings boil over, shocking us, tipping us off balance, and everything becomes a frightening question mark. We feel depleted. Frantic, tense, unable to cope. How does one get off this misery-go-round? Can any good possibly come out of such emotional disarray?

Superwoman. That's what they called me. A friend years before had tagged the name on me. It was meant as a compliment. I could never quite accept it as such. SuperGod would have been more accurate. He it was who had seen me through time after time. I knew I was not capable of superwoman feats. I felt wounded much of the time. Wasn't there a song or a poem that talked about "the bird with the broken pinion"—meaning, of course, that it couldn't fly. I identified. The Superman of the comics could fly—soar away to tremendous heights and perform amazing deeds. I felt as if I were crawling much of the time. It was becoming increasingly difficult to pretend. Superwoman! I knew the tag was a misnomer when applied to me. I longed to shed it.

Our marriage relationship was not what it was supposed to be, and it was taking its toll. Harmony in the home was something we could not seem to achieve, although we both tried. We were Christians; Christians living in a state of undivorce. Hurt was heaped upon hurt. Unresolved differences—a common pattern, I have since discovered, in almost every instance of divorce. The Bible says, "Let not the sun go down upon your wrath" (Eph. 4:26). Apologies. Attempts to clear the air. Bad communication or total lack of it. Failure by one or the other or both time after time after time.

I had read that essential to a woman's happiness in marriage is her human dignity. She cannot suffer hurt, humiliations, insults, or unfair treatment by her mate without damage to her soul. The same book says that in severe cases, love itself can be destroyed. When a wife constantly pushes or nettles her husband, it is like the bite of a poisonous snake and can cause the destruction of a could-be holy marriage. It speaks of a woman losing her husband's love by constant criticisms and attempts to "change" him. But I knew the same thing could happen in reverse. It was happening to me. I knew it was happening to others. I had long sensed that I'd made a mistake as a very immature young woman who had not sought God's clear will and guidance about a life partner.

The word "divorce" began to hover in the back of my mind—an unwelcome guest, an intruder of the worst kind. Divorce! It was such an awful word. You spat it out with contempt if you even so much as had to say it. Divorced people? Anathema. You avoided them; after all, Christians didn't divorce. When you saw people you knew were divorced, you pretended not to see them; you conveniently looked the other way, you maneuvered your grocery shopping cart down another aisle to avoid bumping into them. You went out of your way to avoid a confrontation with a divorced person. What could you say? What do you talk about to divorced people? No, genuine Christians just didn't divorce. Spirit-filled people just couldn't have marital problems. They just didn't have. Divorce? Divorce was unscriptural. Sinful. God couldn't possibly forgive such a gross sin. You clung to the belief that nice Christian people just didn't divorce, and God couldn't countenance it.

Could he?

Or could he? It became a haunting question. Unanswered. And so the search began. What did the Bible really have to say about divorce?

THINK ON THESE THINGS

We are not superwomen or supermen and should not expect superfeats of our fellow Christian brothers or sisters.

What happiness for those whose guilt has been forgiven! What joys when sins are covered over! What relief for those who have confessed their sins and God has cleared their record.

There was a time when I wouldn't admit what a sinner I was. But my dishonesty made me miserable and filled my days with frustration. All day and all night your hand was heavy on me. My strength evaporated like water on a sunny day until I finally admitted all my sins to you and stopped trying to hide them. I said to myself, "I will confess them to the Lord." And you forgave me! All my guilt is gone.

Now I say that each believer should confess his sins to God when he is aware of them, while there is time to be forgiven. Judgment will not touch him if he does.

You are my hiding place from every storm of life; you even keep me from getting into trouble! You surround me with songs of victory. I will instruct you (says the Lord) and guide you along the best pathway for your life; I will advise you and watch your progress. Don't be like a senseless horse or mule that has to have a bit in its mouth to keep it in line!

Many sorrows come to the wicked, but abiding love surrounds those who trust in the Lord. So rejoice in him, all those who are his, and shout for joy, all those who try to obey him (Ps. 32).

3
The Search

The letter came in the mail unsigned. It said, "For the Lord, the God of Israel, says: 'I hate divorce and marital separation' " (Mal. 2:16a, *AB*).

That was all. It was enough. Enough to hurt, that is. Enough to make my already twisting insides twist and turn some more. I knew God hated divorce. Did the anonymous friend who sent the note not believe, could he or she possibly not know, that I had already looked up all the Scripture references on the subject of divorce? Did he or she think I would not consult God's Word? I would give him or her the benefit of the doubt. Perhaps they honestly thought I would ignore what God has said, and they felt it their Christian duty to apprise me of what the Word unmistakably says. "God, help me not to feel bitterness toward that individual. And thank you for your Word, for your whole counsel in the Bible." This was my prayer plea.

Another individual shared with me that after he made the decision to get a divorce, some friends met him following a morning church service, handed him a card listing the references to divorce in the Bible, and said, "God can't bless your ministry for him in the future, you know."

"It was like a kick in the stomach," he said. "Didn't they think I knew what the Bible had to say on the subject? Didn't they realize I was just as aware, perhaps even more so than they, of these specific verses? Would I be so callous and indifferent as not to search this ∩ut.? I really didn't need that from them," he comments, "but I sure could have used some love and understanding. Who needs to be told, 'God can't bless your future ministry for him!' Thank God I knew better. Thank God I had the assurance that he loves me even though I may fail him!"

Yes, I knew what this person was saying. It was an echo of some of my own thoughts.

There are times when we, as God's children, do disobey him, but it does not mean we are no longer his children. No earthly father disowns and ceases to love his disobedient child, unless that father is a tyrannical, unforgiving, totally merciless, unloving father. How much more God, as our all-knowing, understanding, heavenly Father, loves and accepts us when we confess our sinfulness. We are still his children. Disobedience doesn't mean we are no longer sons—our position in him is secure.

God sees the anguish in the divorced person's heart. He reads motives. He knows what has brought us to this place of decision, what has precipitated it, and all that has gone on behind the scenes that others cannot possibly know. God loves us with justice. The book of Romans is strong stuff; it both convicts and comforts. We need both. Many things in life may separate us from friends and family, but nothing can separate us from the love of Christ. His love endures. It is constant and consistent. He does not love us the less for our sinfulness; on the contrary, he stands with us. We can be more than conquerors; not in our own strength, surely through no virtue of our own, but in the great grace and love that God has exhibited in his Son, Jesus.

But what are the verses that deal with divorce in the Bible? What specifically does the Bible say on the subject?

MARRIAGE AND DIVORCE IN THE OLD TESTAMENT

In Genesis 2, verses 18, 20, and 24, the creation narrative is given. Adam was alone; then the Lord God said, "It is not good for the man to be alone, I will make him a helper suitable for him" (vs. 18, *NAS*). The marriage relationship involves the total being, as seen in verse 24 where it says "they shall be one flesh."

The word "divorce" is first mentioned in Deut. 24:1-4. The implication seems to be that divorce on the part of the man was an accepted way of life in the Semitic world. Then as now, however, there was dispute about the reasons why and causes for divorce action. In Old Testament times, the husband definitely had the upper hand.

Israel is pictured symbolically in the Old Testament as being the bride or the wife of Jehovah. In Isaiah 5, for example, we have the song of the lover bewailing the fact that his lover does not love him or follow him. Israel's idolatry showed her constant faithlessness, but the people, it seemed, learned nothing from God's action. Jeremiah, the prophet, pictures God as sending Israel (the northern kingdom) away with a writ of divorce. He says that for all the adulteries of faithless Israel, God has "put her away and given her a bill of divorce" (Jer. 3:8, *AV*). In these ancient times, when the women were divorced their children were sold into slavery. Isaiah 50:1 pictures this tragedy so graphically. "Thus says the Lord, 'Where is the certificate of divorce, By which I have sent your mother away? Or to whom of my creditors did I sell you? Behold, you were sold for your iniquities, And for your transgressions your mother was sent away.' "

Dr. A. Berkeley Mickelsen (a professor of New Testament interpretation) explains this so well by stating that "the implication is that God made no official divorce. He has no creditors to whom he must hand over his sons because of any default on his part. Unfaithfulness, hardness of heart, and many other factors hurt the institution of marriage in Old Testament times. God used the Jews' knowledge of this as a picture of his relationship to them. In his judgment the Lord does discipline, but his hand is not shortened that it cannot redeem" (Isa. 50:2).[1]

In the Book of Hosea, Israel is represented as the adulterous wife of Jehovah. The Lord divorced Israel for good reason, but we see the beautiful picture of the adulteress expiated by her husband, Hosea. Then the Lord said, "Go, and get your wife again and bring her back to you and love her, even though she loves adultery. For the Lord still loves Israel though she has turned to other gods and offered them choice gifts" (Hos. 3:1).

It is in the prophets that we find a more developed picture of divorce. As quoted at the outset of this book, God hates divorce. It is the prophet Malachi who condemns the faithlessness of men to their wives (Mal. 2:14-16). It is in the context of this situation—unfaithfulness—that the prophet so emphatically declares God's hatred of divorce.

MARRIAGE AND DIVORCE IN THE GOSPELS

The unmistakable teaching from the Gospels is that divorce and remarriage for *any* reason are a miscarriage of God's purpose for marriage. Jesus' teachings on this, amplified elsewhere in this book, are to be found in Matt. 5:27-32; 19:3-12; and Mark 10:2-12; with one other allusion to this in Luke 16:18.

Dr. Leighton Ford asks the question, "Can we really expect people to live up to Jesus' teaching?" He answers that by stating: "Can we make Jesus' words into a law for modern pagan society, made up of selfish, secular people? Probably not. Jesus is giving the *ideal*. He is not legislating for society."[2]

In John's Gospel, chapter 4, we see Jesus in action dealing with a woman who was notoriously known in her city for her many marriages and the men in her life. Elsewhere, I discuss this in detail. Clearly, this section shows that although Jesus declared that marriage should be permanent he was aware that for many people it is not. "God wills that men do not lie or steal also, yet lying and stealing exist and are symptoms that men are being ruined by sin."[3] Jesus' dealings with this woman are a beautiful demonstration of his love. Divorce represents failure and leaves scars. But "Jesus' action is a potent protest against legalism—in the complicated questions of divorce we dare not be legalists. We must be concerned with people and how they can best put their lives back together again by God's power and help."[4]

Marriage and Divorce in the Epistles

In Rom. 7:1-3, we have a picture of women under Jewish law. Their status was difficult from the legalistic perspective. Paul actually uses this illustration to show how, before Christ, we were bound to and held captive by the law with all its demands and commands. But thanks be to God, in belonging to Christ, the Christian, Paul says, has been released from the law, having died to that by which we were bound, so that we "serve in newness of the Spirit and not in the oldness of the letter" (Rom. 7:6, *AV*).

In 1 Corinthians, chapter 7, Paul spells out his feelings in great detail about marriage, what we today would call "single bliss," the separation of Christian marriage partners, marriage between a Christian and an unbeliever, and his concern about the times in which they were living. Paul's statements on marriage, however, do not cover all the complexities that arise in marital situations. There are many gaps in what happens inside the four walls of a home that neither Jesus nor Paul touch upon. What both Jesus and Paul are doing is to set up the ideal, urging followers to strive to attain to this.

Many marriages are deeply hurt by personal idiosyncrasies in individual partners, which may not show up in courtship days. These problems and habits carried over into a marriage can destroy love and the marriage itself. This is sin, but where sin is not admitted, confessed, and dealt with, the marriage relationship can be hurt and greatly jeopardized. Very few Christians, I fear, would take Paul's words in Gal. 6:1 and apply them to the complex problem of divorce among fellow Christians. Here Paul urges, "Brethren, even if a man is caught in any trespass, you who are spiritual, restore such a one in a spirit of gentleness; looking to yourself, lest you too be tempted" (*NAS*).

In Eph. 5:21-33, we see what should be the attitude of wives and husbands in marriage. The model given is Christ's relationship to the church. No better blueprint for being a genuinely changed partner in marriage can be found than right here in this passage of Scripture. This could rightly be called the Apostle Paul's prescription for a happy marriage.

> Be subject to one another in the fear of Christ.
>
> Wives, be subject to your own husbands, as to the Lord.
>
> For the husband is the head of the wife, as Christ also is the head of the church, He Himself being the Savior of the body.
>
> But as the church is subject to Christ, so also the wives ought to be to their husbands in everything.
>
> Husbands, love your wives, just as Christ also loved the church and gave Himself up for her;
>
> that He might sanctify her, having cleansed her by the washing of water with the word,
>
> that He might present to Himself the church in all her glory, having no spot or wrinkle or any such thing; but that she should be holy and blameless.
>
> So husbands ought also to love their own wives as their own bodies. He who loves his own wife loves himself;
>
> for no one ever hated his own flesh, but nourishes and cherishes it, just as Christ also does the church, because we are members of His body.

For this cause a man shall leave his father and mother, and shall cleave to his wife; and the two shall become one flesh.

This mystery is great; but I am speaking with reference to Christ and the church.

Nevertheless let each individual among you also love his own wife even as himself; and let the wife see to it that she respect her husband (*NAS*).

Evangelist Leighton Ford says:

Sometimes it's said marriage is a 50-50 proposition. Don't you believe it! Of course, in one sense a good marriage has to include giving in and adjusting to each other in many ways, big and small. But at the heart, marriage is no 50-50 deal. It's 100 percent give both ways. That's what Paul was driving at when he said what he did in Ephesians 5.[5]

Today much is being written and said in a disparaging way regarding women being submissive to men. The feminist movement has done much to encourage rebellion among the ranks of females, encouraging instead equality with men. It is acknowledged that the greater freedom that is being accorded to women has led to more of them seeking divorce. But the Christian woman who understands what Ephesians 5 is saying and her role as it relates to her husband has no difficulty in submission when her husband also understands and accepts what this passage is saying.

The trouble arises when both partners fail to grasp the real significance of what the Apostle Paul is saying. He is not giving license to husbands to lord it over their wives in a demanding, repulsive way. In this passage there is a very fine balance between the right attitude, and the desired action on the part of both husbands and wives. If the Spirit of God would indwell completely the heart of each partner in marriage, then there would be no abrasiveness; each would look to the greater happiness and best welfare of the other. That's why it is no 50-50 deal, but 100 percent giving both ways!

I can conceive of no woman seeking a divorce when her husband is doing what Ephesians 5 says—loving her as Christ loved the Church ("He gave his very life to take care of it and be its Savior!" vs. 23). That kind of loving can only call forth a willing, loving response from a man's wife.

How many people who react so violently to the idea of divorce among Christians recognize that the wife is not receiving that kind of treatment from her husband? This is another side of divorce that is rarely presented.

In the same way, how many wives are accepting their husband's leadership and obeying him lovingly so as to prompt him to treat her lovingly? Or are they indulging in self-pity, nagging, being unreasonable—setting up all sorts of barriers to an expression from him of the kind of love the Bible enjoins him to give?

If a husband is to receive his wife's respect, however, he must earn it. The Bible tells him how to do it—by loving her as he loves himself. When a husband fails in this regard, he is adulterating their marriage relationship. He is to give his wife the same gracious care the Lord Jesus Christ has given to us as the Savior of the body. It is God's intent that every Christian home should exemplify this very thing.

Kenneth Taylor in *The Living Bible* makes this concept very plain when he says "a man is really doing himself a favor and loving himself when he loves his wife!" (Eph. 5:28b). He concludes the passage this way: "So again I say, a man must love his wife as a part of himself; and the wife must see to it that she deeply respects her husband—obeying, praising and honoring him" (vs. 32).

THINK ON THESE THINGS

Christian world, do not judge me, and do not judge other divorced Christians. Remember, you have not walked in our moccasins, nor have we walked in yours.

> For the Lord grants wisdom! His every word is a treasure of knowledge and understanding. He grants good sense to the godly—his saints. He is their shield, protecting them and guarding their pathway (Prov. 2:6–8).

4
The Whole Counsel of God

It was tough to take. The Bible is very plain. It can hurt. When you love the Lord and love his Word, the truth hurts. You don't deny his Word, argue with it, rationalize, or try to squirm around it. You accept it. You seek to live by it. This is God speaking. He is your Heavenly Father. You want to be his obedient child. And yet your heart cries out for peace and happiness. You know that personal happiness is not to be the supreme goal in life, but you do crave for a measure of love and peace.

Peace. How many there are who are searching for that very thing! The Bible says God hath called us to live in peace (1 Cor. 7:15). It also says that Jesus is our way of peace (Eph. 2:14).

We live in a real world with very real problems. Where did we ever get the idea that Christians are to be immune from marital problems? The issues of life that cause turmoil and unpeace in the non-Christian's life are very much a part of the Christian's experience also. We are not exempt from the effects of sin—and those of us who are victims of divorce would be the first to admit and recognize that divorce is the result of the perversity of human nature and sin. The Christian has resources at his disposal that the non-Christian does not recognize and is not using. But having said that, there must still come the recognition that marital turmoil exists and can result in divorce.

I was faced with the reality of my problems daily upon

awakening. I still am. And so are you, if you are going to be honest with yourself and God. God is not the cosmic problem solver that some would portray him to be. I recognize that he is all-powerful, but there are those who would throw everything onto him and refuse to accept their responsibility. God chooses to equip his children to solve their problems and to be able to face life drawing from him the resources that will give them the power. The Bible says here on earth we will have many trials and sorrows (John 16:33), but that we are to cheer up, for he (Jesus) has overcome the world.

The Bible also says we are to cast all our care upon him, for he cares for us (1 Pet. 5:7). Many marriages, however, are so totally destructive to the individuals concerned that the only way to successfully cast one's care upon him is by taking action to come out from under that which is so oppressively weighing one down. Spiritual growth is hampered when all of one's energies and strength are being expended for mere survival, just to keep one's head above water and to maintain one's sanity. In the final analysis the possibility exists and I have seen it happen—and so have you if you will stop to think—that both people can come out of a divorce with far more insight, spiritual strength, and understanding, because the negative evaluations, criticisms, and living in a state of constant upheaval and discontent have been removed—all factors which contribute to the prohibition of spiritual growth.

Have you ever thought that it takes courage to face divorce? When you look at divorced persons, have you ever looked at them with the thought that they are courageous? I fear that most Christians regard divorced people with something less than thoughts like that; on the contrary, they are mostly regarded as backing out of a difficult situation, selfish possibly, unreasonable, seeking an out, an escape from their responsibilities, unwilling to seek God's will and to draw upon him, to follow his leading, or to cast all the cares and problems upon him. But to face divorce does take courage; for some of us it took more courage than to maintain the pretense of a happy marriage and live a lie.

When I finally decided upon divorce, it came as a result of an unwillingness to continue living a lie. I knew that God saw my heart. I wasn't fooling him. It troubled me. I'd read it many times, and every time I stumbled over the words that God sees not as man sees, for man looks at the outward appearance, but the Lord looks at the heart (1 Sam. 16:7b). God saw me as I really was. God saw the marital situation as it really was. I may have fooled our friends and the church; those who knew me, read my books, or heard me speak might not know that I had a troubled heart; *but God knew.*

I wanted to live as openly before the world as I was living before God. This became the determining factor as I recognized that man judgeth after the flesh (John 8:15); but that it was God alone who was my real judge. But he was also my loving Heavenly Father, and I would throw myself upon his mercy. Romans 9 assured me that God's blessings are not given just because someone decides to have them or works hard to get them. They are given because God takes pity on those he wants to.

We try to compress God into our own little molds. He's a big God, and sometimes he moves in strange ways, and you cannot doubt him. God hates divorce, but he hates other things as well. He loves justice and hates robbery and wrong (Isa. 61:8). There is what has often been referred to as the "Hate Parade" in Prov. 6:16–19. Here we are told that there are seven things the Lord hates; they are an abomination to him: (1) haughtiness, a proud look; (2) lying; (3) murdering, hands that shed innocent blood; (4) plotting evil, a heart that deviseth wicked imaginations; (5) eagerness to do wrong— feet that are swift in running to mischief; (6) a false witness that speaketh lies; and (7) sowing discord among brethren.

It was beginning to dawn on me; the Bible is a big book. Rich and full. I knew what it said about living in unpeace. I knew what it said about divorce. But it also had much to say about other things God hates. Why should divorced people be singled out? I asked the question repeatedly. I even had a vivid dream in which there was to be a purge throughout the Christian church. The purge began with all those who were divorced. But then a surprising thing happened—God was calling for honesty. The judge of the universe sought for honest people, and those who wished they were divorced were asked to step forward. I turned my head in that dream. I closed my eyes. I avoided looking. My own insides ached and had ached so often in the past. Now, in my dream, my insides ached for my brothers and sisters in the Lord, many of whom I knew were living in unhappy marital states, some of whom had expressed their feelings about wishing they dared divorce. The hurt I had often felt in the past had even manifested itself in physical symptoms that were extremely painful, some requiring hospitalization. I hurt for others like that in the dream.

If we are going to be consistent in our Christian institutions and churches, then let us have a purge of all undesirable elements to be found within our ranks. Who would be left? In many Christian groups we have already labeled and excluded divorced people, and especially those who remarry or wish to remarry. But let us follow through and pass equally harsh judgment upon those who gossip (the book of James has a great deal to say about the tongue, doesn't it?). Let the purge of Christendom also include those who lie, steal, are proud, and the other things the Bible clearly states that God hates. Such a purge would even have to include those who overindulge in eating, for the Bible contains strong words regarding gluttony and drinking. If the Old Testament law were to be followed exactly, then those who are stubborn or rebellious would have to be turned away from fellowship. But sin is sin, and the list of sins God hates could go on and on. Divorce is one of them, of that there can be no doubt; yet the Bible has much to say on these other sins as well—in some instances more is said on certain other sins than on the subject of divorce—but divorced people are singled out. Many times they are excommunicated, denied the sacraments deprived of church positions, and pressure is brought to bear upon them in harsh and obvious ways.

My self-esteem had been dealt a severe blow, but I did what I had done so often in the past; I turned to the Bible and looked at the lives of some of the biblical people. A Greek sage once said that the proper study of mankind is man. It had always made good sense to me to look at those whose lives have been so faithfully recorded for us in God's Word. Jesus' love for the fallible Peter was a source of great encouragement. As I looked at Peter and others, I saw that their failures were as frankly dealt with as their successes. Certainly their failures were not glossed over. I looked at Peter and took courage.

Would you or I have chosen this simple, impulsive, impetuous one to be the leader of the apostolic band? I doubt it. And right there we have an important lesson on the folly of our trying to judge others and decide what is right or wrong for them to do. We'd have called Peter a failure, based on his actions. He was so volcanic, so inconsistent, so undisciplined. His speech was rash, and he made hasty decisions— often making horrible mistakes. Peter was outspoken and inclined to some instability. He definitely had what we today might label fatal flaws in his character.

Peter's blunderings, however, afforded Jesus marvelous opportunities to teach Peter (and us) valuable lessons. In spite of weakness and obvious failure, this man was eager, courageous—even though at one point he temporarily panicked and denied Jesus, still he had depth and genuineness of love. While Peter's heart often ruled his head, this big, big heart was anxious to follow Christ, so willing to be taught, and humbly honest.

Do you know that Peter received more rebukes from Jesus than any other disciple? He didn't want Jesus to wash his feet;

he made an irresponsible suggestion on the Mount of Transfiguration; he boasted of superior courage—but Jesus saw into Peter's heart. He looked beyond these momentary failures and saw a man passionately devoted to him. And Peter was willing to learn. He saw his own fallibility and weakness and admitted it to Jesus. Jesus, with comforting insight and love, restored him with great forgiveness.

Jesus never gave up on Peter. I do not believe Jesus gives up on divorced people. What encouragement this is for those of us who feel we fail Christ so miserably at times!

Peter wept bitterly. Many divorced individuals have confided to me how often they have wept. Jesus takes note of every tear. The psalmist said that God saw him tossing and turning and collected all his tears and preserved them in his bottle, recording every one in his book (Ps. 56:8). The psalmist went on to say:

> This one thing *I know: God is for me!* I am trusting God—oh, praise His promises! I am not afraid of anything mere man can do to me. Yes, praise His promises. For You have saved me from death and my feet from slipping, so that I can walk before the Lord in the land of the living (vs. 9b–13).

As long as we live in the land of the living, we are going to be faced with difficult decisions, personality clashes, and experiences that will send us to our knees in tears. The most poignant tears are those wept over sin and a recognition of our own failure.

After Jesus patiently dealt with Peter, he drew from him the confession, "I love thee." Jesus didn't extract from Peter a promise for better performance in the future, or that he would never fail him again; but he looked into the intent of Peter's heart, saw his thoughts, and gave to Peter the commission to "feed my lambs and feed my sheep."

I couldn't help but think of my friend who, while in the

process of getting a divorce, was told, "God can't bless your ministry for him in the future, you know." What if Jesus had said that to Peter! Thank God he didn't!

But Jesus went a step further. He entrusted to Peter the keys of the kingdom of heaven. He gave power to Peter, Holy Spirit power. But Peter was not the first nor the last to receive that kind of power. I saw that same power fall upon my friend. I felt that same power move in my life. Thank God for the likes of Peter stumbling his way through the pages of the Gospels. Peter's transformation powerfully demonstrates that God can lift us from failure to new heights of usefulness for him. He can take us through our deep-water experiences, anguish, and suffering and help us as we relate to others, seeking to show them the whole counsel of God.

I am convinced that God would have us identify with the Bible people. Their experiences can help us over the hurdles and obstacles that come our way. We, too, can channel our experiences constructively as we come to terms with past marital failure but recognize that this does not have to characterize the future for us. We will encounter conflicting emotions along the way of adjustment, but this is an important part of our personal growth into healthy thinking, independent individuals who are acting and responding to circumstances instead of reacting according to the dictates of mates with whom we differed on almost everything.

I know of no Christian who, having made the agonizing decision to obtain a divorce, hasn't done so only after hours of searching the Scripture, seeking the whole counsel of God, praying and waiting on him; then, on the very realistic side of the whole tragic business, hasn't done all he or she could to hold the marriage together. (I am referring specifically to those divorced Christians whom I interviewed for this book.) Has God's hand of blessing been removed? Has he shown himself to be unmerciful and unforgiving? Has he not given peace?

Think on These Things

A divorced woman said, "This town is like Noah's Ark: if you aren't part of a pair, they shut you out." Is your town, your church comfortable only with married couples? If divorce is a sin, since when has the church decided to exclude sinners? Divorced singles exist within the community and more than likely within your church. Acting on the whole counsel of God, can *you* accept them in positive practical ways? Do you presently have a singles group in your church? Does the need exist for one to begin? How can you help? Beyond such helping, how can you personally show that you care, that there is acceptance and love?

Trust yourself to the God who made you, for He will never fail you (1 Pet. 4:19b).

5
Peace

Divorce is essentially a funeral ceremony, the ritual in our culture in which the dead marriage of living partners is buried. But divorce can become a living endless death when forgiveness is withheld by the very ones who should be holding out understanding, encouragement, and love. We can also prolong the agony of mourning for ourselves when we refuse to come to terms with our own contribution to the failure of the marriage and do something about self-defeating behavior. We are often our own worst enemies.

The *Los Angeles Times*[1] carried an article on the need for marital counseling and said of divorce that it is a burial ceremony. A relationship has died, and you have to bury it somewhere. The same article said that divorce is an opportunity for growth. These were the varying viewpoints of a lawyer, a psychologist, a court official, and a social welfare authority. If what is generally called the non-Christian world can regard divorce as an opportunity for growth, why can't the Christian world (even though we recognize that it is not the ideal way to grow)?

The wounds divorce inflicts upon its victims are, I believe, some of the most cruel. The pain is deep and terribly real, and often wounds that have just begun to heal are mercilessly ripped open by the biting sarcasm or hurtful acts and words of others. I am sorry to have to say that, but it is distressingly true. This is verified in the many conversations I have had with divorced individuals. I marvel at their lack of bitterness.

One man said, "I am the only one who gets hurt when I allow bitterness to take root." Seldom have I observed so mellow a character as this man evidenced. I myself am of the opinion that the hard experiences of life can do one of two things to us—they will make us either better or bitter. The choice is up to us.

Another individual said, "I've had to learn to roll with the punches." But I find myself asking: Why should fellow Christians be punching at someone who has already been knocked down?

In some instances there is a tinge of bitterness. I believe it is to be expected—think back in your own experiences when you've faced difficulties. When it exists, however, I have seen the individuals quickly identify it, acknowledge it for what it is, and express concern and a desire to rid themselves of it. I think of my own experience many times over when this happened. How faithful God is! A case in point may help the reader to identify.

"It's between you and God," said a well-meaning friend whom I chanced to meet at a restaurant. There was no mistaking it, her entire attitude betrayed the fact that this is what she was really thinking. What she was saying (to herself) was, "You're doing a sinful thing and God is going to judge you, and as far as I'm concerned, he's already judged you to hell!" She walked off, head held high, before I had a chance to tell her I thought she was correct—that it was between God and myself. I've never heard from her since. Oh, but you are perhaps saying, now who's judging? And why didn't you make an effort to call her? She had made it plain that she considered what I was doing was completely wrong and that unless I changed my mind I was tainted and our friendship was terminated. One hesitates to call someone in a situation like that. I harbor no grudges toward her and others who may react in a similar way. I feel great sympathy for them. They cannot be living at peace with themselves and God. I long to reach out and tell them I understand and that if we will but allow God to judge and deal with others in his way, we ourselves will be far better off.

God charts the blueprint for our lives, so who are we, mere humans, to try and pencil in the direction we think another's life should go? For the most part, the divorced people whom I talked to and the many pastors and professional people who have shared counseling experiences relate a sweetened spirit, a softened attitude, a Christlike growth, and a sense of peace.

Mental and physical anguish is often compounded, however, by sincere Christians who feel duty-bound to offer advice "meant for your own good," as they state. I do not doubt their sincerity, nor do I fault them for it. But how often we forget or bypass the biblical injunctions to show mercy to those suffering the agonies of painful circumstances that seem all out of step with the generally accepted Christian mode of doing things.

Divorced individuals experience alternate feelings of deep depression, guilt, anger, hate, and hostility, but on the other side of the coin, a vast sense of relief and peace.

Yes, peace. When you have lived in an unpeaceful situation, to be freed from that brings with it an accompanying sense of real peace. In my own case, having prayed earnestly for guidance and having put out a "fleece" and experiencing a definite answer, I found refuge in Isa. 26:3, *AV.* "Thou wilt keep him in perfect peace, whose mind is stayed on Thee: because he trusteth in Thee." That which most often generated feelings of unpeace came, sadly, from others.

"Brethren, these things ought not to be." I could hear the Apostle Paul's words. Perhaps I was too naïve. Is it possible to be too trusting? I was trusting in the whole counsel of God. I expected the same expressions of understanding and love from my fellow Christians. Isn't this what the Bible commands? In Eph. 4:32, *AV*, we read: "Be ye kind one to another, tenderhearted, forgiving one another, even as God for Christ's sake hath forgiven you."

Several divorced Christians said they believed many in the

Christian community take divorced people to the whipping post. Added to their heartache are verbal lashings and tongue abuse heaped upon them by those who comprise the body of Christ. This is not an indictment against all Christians per se; but it is to report the fact that this does exist as shared with me by those who have experienced it.

Can the divorced Christian then live in peace? Yes, emphatically so! There are many divorced Christians who are remarried who are keeping the fact that they were divorced at one time a secret. They are afraid to expose the fact that one or both of them have been divorced. Why? For fear the peace and newfound joy they are experiencing will be spoiled somehow. There are many others who are fearlessly facing up to the facts, living outright and letting it be known that they have been divorced. The first group is not to be condemned. The stigma is real, especially where there is remarriage. I have sympathetic understanding for them but believe greater peace and joy would be their portion if they, too, did not feel it was necessary to conceal the truth. I have personally made the beautiful discovery that when I level with people it is almost as if they breathe a sigh of relief when they discover, as one young woman said, "She's human, too!"

Divorced Christians share many things in common, not the least of which is this feeling of deep inner peace that comes once they have weathered the initial criticism, the shock of their Christian contemporaries, and accompanying trauma. *We have learned that Christ can be taken at his Word.*

It has been proven that next to the death of a loved one, divorce is one of the most traumatic experiences of a lifetime.

Mel Krantzler, who has written an eye-opening book on divorce, sees divorce as a new opportunity for personal growth. It is his belief that

> the death of a relationship is the first stage in a process in which the relationship is mourned and then laid to rest

to make way for self-renewal. It is a crisis that must be lived through. More than that, however, more than just a time for picking up the pieces, divorce is a new opportunity to improve on the past and create a fuller life.[2]

I did not recognize at first in my own experience the fact that divorced people go through a period of mourning, much as we do when we lose a loved one in actual death. The relationship with all its associations, attachments, and memories has been severed; therefore it is synonymous with an actual death. It took me some time to realize that the mourning process is natural and therapeutic. At first I resented my conflicting emotions. What was I mourning anyway? Wasn't I glad to be out of a situation that was so destructive to both of us? I believe now that the Christian who is sensitive to the Holy Spirit, who wants so very much to be kind, tender-hearted, and understanding, experiences a particular type of grief that can best be explained as mourning over the fact that you feel you have grieved the Son of God most of all. As I faced my emotions, ventilating my feelings through prayerful reaching out to God, writing my thoughts out, and talking them over with wonderful Christian friends, I was able to work through the situation to a point where once again I felt physiological and emotional balance was restored. Always my Bible was near at hand, and I retreated into the Psalms, particularly, where I felt close to David, who also experienced great highs and lows.

While researching for a writing assignment during the immediate post-divorce days, I came across something in Mark 4 which helped me tremendously. Jesus and his disciples were standing by the lake. It had been a busy day of ministering and teaching the immense crowds which always followed him. As evening fell, Jesus said to his disciples, "Let's cross to the other side of the lake" (vs. 35). Nothing particularly unusual about that—Jesus and his disciples did that frequently. But as I looked at the scene, trying to picture it in my mind's eye as I read on, I saw that as they entered the boat and started out a terrible storm arose.

Common sense dictates that if the sky is black, if storm clouds are hanging low, and it appears that it's going to rain, you'd best stay out of a boat and keep to dry land and the safety of the shore until the storm blows over. Was the sky really stormy? We do not know; the Bible is silent. Sometimes storms arise very suddenly with little or no warning; other times a storm is predictable. How would you like to get in a boat, I said to myself, if the sky was dark and a storm threatened on the horizon? Count me out, was my immediate reply.

But the disciples did enter the boat with Jesus. And soon there arose a fierce gale of wind, so much so that the waves were breaking over the boat until it was nearly full and they were about to sink (vs. 35–41). Where was Jesus? "Jesus was asleep at the back of the boat with his head on a cushion" (vs. 38).

That stopped me short. Where was Jesus while this storm was raging in my life? I remembered the occasion when one of our children had asked me, "Mama, does God ever sleep?" At that time I had told him that God never slept, that he was ever watchful of his children. "Honey," I had said, "God always keeps his children safe. He doesn't need sleep. He's God! We don't understand it, but we don't need to. We just know. And, we just love him that much more. The Bible tells us that God keeps us and he never sleeps, 'for he is always watching, never sleeping' " (Ps. 121:3–4).

Yes, God is the bodyguard of his saints. Did I believe it? Can you? We do Christ a great wrong when we suspect him of being careless about his people in distress. My mind went back to the episode with Jesus and his disciples on the storm-tossed lake. What did the fearful disciples do? They awoke him, of course! Frantically they shouted, "Teacher, don't you even care that we are all about to drown?" (vs. 38).

Then Jesus rebuked the wind and said to the raging sea,

"Quiet down. Peace, be still" (vs. 39). Immediately the wind ceased, and there was a great calm. Then Jesus looked at his trembling disciples and rebuked them. "Why were you so fearful? Don't you even yet have confidence in me?" (vs. 40).

I, too, felt rebuked. It is true that circumstances may toss us about quite a bit and we may seem at our wits' end, but we are not at our faith's end when we have such a loving Savior to whom we can turn. I remembered reading that someone had suggested that the disciples could have shouted in the face of the storm. *They* could have said to the raging winds and rolling waves, "Peace, be still. You can do us no harm, for Christ, the mighty Savior, is on board!"

What a lesson! The Master Teacher was once again driving home a lesson to this pupil. It's much easier to trust when the sun is shining than when the storm is raging; who among us would deny that? But we do have the power of Christ at our command. We are not powerless. Can we learn that with Christ in the vessel *we* can smile through the storm? Christ had said to his disciples, "Let us go to the other side." He had not said to them, "Let us go to the middle of the lake and be drowned in a storm."

Peace. Even in the midst of life's stormy situations? Even in the midst of divorce? That ship which has Christ on board—that individual who has Christ living within—may be tossed but will not sink. Regardless how severe the storm of trouble, it is God's prerogative to command the situation. He who made the seas can make them quiet. It is by looking to him, listening to hear him say, "Peace, be still," that *we* experience a great calm.

THINK ON THESE THINGS

In our emotions divorce produces a *separation* shock which can equal in intensity the feelings evoked by the actual death of a husband or wife; and it sets in motion reactions similar to those which an actual death can cause: initial denial that the relationship has ended, producing at first a retreat into a fantasy life where it can still live on; powerful feelings of hostility and anger toward the absent person for having abandoned us to an intolerable life without him or her; pervasive feelings of guilt, internalized or projected, over things we did and didn't do during our relationship; a withdrawal from those parts of our past too painful to cope with (or too irrelevant to survive in our present lives); a gradual testing and retesting of reality; and an eventual letting-go from the influence of the past relationship so that a new life can begin.

These elements of mourning are inherent in each divorce, but the mixture and intensity of the stages vary widely, since no two individuals are the same. We bring to our divorce experience the sum total of our strengths and weaknesses as human beings, along with the unique world view our past history has given to us.[3]

Out of all of this—given the opportunity by others, and a willingness on the part of one's self, the divorced individual can emerge stronger, better equipped to accept the challenges of the present, open to whatever God may have in the future.

"Wherefore be ye not unwise, but understanding what the will of the Lord is" (Eph. 5:17, *AV*).

"Let us therefore follow after the things which make for peace, and things wherewith one may edify another" (Rom. 14:19, *AV*).

6
"Never Get a Divorce!"

Had I heard correctly? I asked him to repeat it. Over the phone, with thousands of miles separating us, I heard distinctly, "It would be better for you to end up in a mental institution than to get a divorce."

Always before, even though we were in different parts of the country, I had felt a nearness to this Christian brother and a great bond of love. Now, suddenly, it was as if the connection was severed. But his voice continued, "Get a separation—a legal separation. But *never get a divorce*."

"It would be better for you to end up in a mental institution than to get a divorce. . . . Never get a divorce." The words hit me with typhoon force.

What would happen to my children if their mother ended up in a mental institution? Is that where God wanted me? Of what use would I be to my family or God in a mental institution? Questions!

Marcie Greenberg, a former member of the California Governor's Commission on the Family and the State Social Welfare Board, was quoted in the *Los Angeles Times* as stating that separate maintenance is a thing of the past and temporary separation lessens the chances for reconciliation. Temporary separation is "horrible for children," Mrs. Greenberg said.[1]

Meyer Elkin, supervising counselor, Conciliation Court, Los Angeles Superior Court, said that although separation can occasionally cool hostility or help fearful people get out of divorce, the longer the separation, the less chances there are for reconciliation unless the partners are being counseled.[2]

In our situation, as with the other people whom I interviewed, counseling had been sought; friends did offer help and advice. But there were children to consider. I could not be a fit mother in a mental institution (and that's exactly where I felt I was headed); nor could I be a fit mother in the state in which our marriage was functioning. I knew what the psalmist meant when he cried out, "My flesh and my heart faileth: but God is the strength of my heart, and my portion for ever. . . . It is good for me to draw near to God: I have put my trust in the Lord God" (Ps. 73:26, 28, *AV*). There are those who will deny that God would counsel anyone to seek divorce; certainly this is not in his perfect will for his children, but in my heart I knew that God's ways are the ways of peace (1 Cor. 7:15b), and the divorce was obtained. I knew that God alone would have to be my counselor. Psalm 73 told me, "Thou shalt guide me with Thy counsel, and afterward receive me to glory" (vs. 24, *AV*).

When talking with divorced individuals while researching this book, I said, "Spare the unpleasant details; they are unimportant. It is between you, your former mate, and God." I really meant that. No divorced person is obligated to stand in defense of himself or herself when challenged and reveal facts that are no one else's business. It is usually stated by Christians that no one person is responsible for marital discord or the breakup of a marriage. What is left unsaid, however, and generally not acknowledged, is the fact that a person's childhood, the relationship an individual had with his or her parents, is a major contributing factor that predetermines his feelings and reactions to the opposite sex in an adult relationship. This can have a devastating effect in a marital relationship. There is much involved that does not meet the eye of the casual observer and those outside the intimacy of the family situation. There are extenuating circumstances that do not surface and show to outsiders, but that only manifest themselves between the two individuals involved; therefore, we are well advised not to interfere or to try and analyze, and judge.

It is also known that many Christians will not accept the findings and recommendations of trained counselors, psychologists, and psychiatrists; but there is much beyond the comprehension of the untrained mind, which often only a professional can understand, and the Christian public must come to grips with and be sensitive to and acknowledge the capabilities of such as these. There are no simplistic answers to the complicated issues that arise in marriages that are less than ideal, and to say that those who do divorce have not turned it over to the Lord and trusted him to work out the situation is to display an ignorance of the total picture as it actually exists.

Under normal circumstances, however, I believe it is quite safe to say that *if a marriage relationship is what it should be to begin with,* no one else can pose a threat to or break up a marriage. The emphasis must be upon the word *normal,* however.

Often, too, there are those why try to pinpoint blame. "She stepped out on him," someone will say; or "He was unfaithful to her." Who has betrayed whom? Who really is "the innocent party"? If a man is receiving a banquet at home, why should he go elsewhere to get crumbs in a clandestine relationship? (This is not referring to their sexual relationship only.) If a woman is being treated as she should be by her spouse, why should she risk everything and search elsewhere for understanding, appreciation, and love? If either one is so demeaning the other with a constant barrage of words, undermining their self-confidence and feeling of worth, is it any wonder that they seek solace in the arms of another who knows how to restore self-confidence and make him feel like a man or her feel like a worthy woman?

On this subject, Dr. Lars Granberg, an eminent counselor and psychologist, says:

A comment on the idea of the "innocent party" seems in order. Any experienced pastor knows that it is rare that such a term is more than relative. Married life is an intricate tapestry of interwoven actions and reactions. Both parties usually contribute to misunderstanding, each in his own way. Hence the pastor is well advised to listen long and carefully and be slow to apportion blame. The more obvious offense is not necessarily the greater.[3]

This is a statement that bears repeating: *The more obvious offense is not necessarily the greater.* Let the critics of that one who is considered the offending partner stop and reflect seriously on that comment.

James Montgomery Boice, writing in *Eternity* magazine, said:

Marriage is for life. But not all marriages attain this permanence. Again and again we are faced with the problems of estrangement, separation, divorce and remarriage. What is the Christian's position in these difficult and tragic situations? Is divorce a permissible option for the Christian? Is it entirely forbidden, or are there conditions under which it is allowable?[4]

The Christian recognizes that God's ideal is that marriage is for life. "What therefore God hath joined together, let not man put asunder" (Matt. 19:6, *AV*). This is discussed in greater detail elsewhere in this book. God himself instituted the relationship between a man and a woman in the state of innocence in the Garden of Eden. Marriage, therefore, is one of the most ancient of divine ordinances. One of the first things that God ever said was *not* good is that man should be alone (Gen. 2:18). Seeing this aloneness, God made a helpmeet for man, a companion suited to his needs (vs. 18b).

One cannot help but wonder, however, how many marriages are instituted where consideration is *not* given to whether or not the man and woman are good for each other, whether they are, in fact, suited to the needs of the other. Many parents have pleaded with their sons and daughters not to marry someone, "You aren't right for each other; you just aren't suitable. . . ." These words usually fall on deaf ears. From the vantage point of maturity, with years of experience behind them, many adults have tried to point the way to younger people about to embark upon the serious sea of matrimony, only to find their pleas ignored and scorned. It is not surprising, then, that many marriages fail, for the Bible admonishes that we heed the wise and loving counsel of parents and those who have our best interests at heart. "Children, obey your parents in the Lord: for this is right. Honour thy father and mother; which is the first commandment with promise; That it may be well with thee, and thou mayest live long on the earth" (Eph. 6:1-3, *AV*).

Perhaps there is value in the ancient Eastern custom, still observed in some parts of the world today, where marriages are arranged by parents. Bishop K. C. Pillai, D.D., a native of India, born into a Hindu home and reared and educated in the rich Eastern tradition, a convert to Christianity, in his fascinating book *Light through an Eastern Window*[5] comments that in spite of the seeming lack of freedom of choice involved in the Oriental system of marriage customs, there is a notable lack of divorce.

It cannot be disputed that God's *perfect* plan is, just as it was in the beginning, that one man love and marry one woman and that these two should not separate until death. Adam and Eve's becoming one flesh was consummated by the will of God. It has always been the divine intention that when two people who are believers unite in marriage, such a union will receive his blessing. Quite possibly what we are seeing in divorce among Christians today is the fact that the individuals involved did not seek God's will, though they may have thought they were acting as Christians. As they mature and grow, there comes the recognition that they didn't know what being a Christian meant after all.

Dr. Jack MacArthur, writing in the pamphlet *Marriage and Divorce*[6] says that if we are going to apply the New Testament teaching to marriage, then we can only apply it in the case of those whom God has joined together. There are multitudes of marriages today that are completely pagan. We can safely say that God had nothing to do with the arrangement and that his perfect will was never sought.

The Apostle Paul amplifies on this idea in 1 Cor. 7:15, where he speaks of unbelieving partners in marriage. In 2 Cor. 6:14, he strongly admonishes that we be not unequally yoked together. The idea is that being teamed up with and bound together with an unbeliever is a horrible mistake that can only lead to heartbreak and heartache. Picture a farmer hitching up a cow and a horse together to plow his field. It is an absurdity.

If this book does nothing more, let it show to the young person contemplating marriage the necessity of seeking God's will about one's life partner, marrying a believer, and then entering into the holy relationship totally committed to the Lord. Two believers with God's blessing on their marriage are beginning in the right way. *Then let these two partners follow the Biblical injunctions as to the husband's role and the wife's responsibility, both seeking unselfishly to live for each other and in the will of God.*

As one thinks about the tragedy of divorce, the disruption caused in the lives of family members who cannot help but be involved and friends who stand by grieved and troubled, there comes the recognition that what God said was surely for our own good. God's laws are for our benefit; Christianity has not only the best interests but the greatest possible happiness at heart for those who embrace it.

Divorce is undesirable. But in dealing with people where they are, even as we look at the biblical ideal regarding the permanence of marriage, and even as we reckon with what my friend said over the phone—"Never get a divorce"—we also must look at Jesus while he walked here upon this earth.

The thought struck me forcibly one morning while lying in bed; just think, Jesus actually did walk here upon earth. He was a living, breathing reality. As I concentrated on that, I visualized him moving in and out among the people of his day. People are people, and they must have been very much like us today. And I saw him constantly meeting people where they were. Right where they were. The Bible confirms this. He's still doing that today, though not in visible form; his Spirit is very much a reality.

Think on These Things

Would Jesus have told the woman at the well that it would have been better for her to end up in a mental institution than to be divorced?

> Give a warm welcome to any brother who wants to join you. . . . Don't criticize him for having different ideas from yours about what is right and wrong. . . . For God has accepted them to be his children. They are God's servants, not yours. They are responsible to him, not to you. Let him tell them whether they are right or wrong. And God is able to make them do as they should (Rom. 14:1, 3b, 4).

7
Jesus and a Divorcée

It is an undeniable fact that Jesus always met people at their point of deepest need. You cannot read the Gospels without recognizing that Jesus, during his life on earth, always responded to the needs of people about him. Oftentimes he would travel out of his way for an encounter with an individual. His sensitivity to the needs in the hearts of people strikes a responsive chord in our own hearts.

In John 4 there is an arresting statement: "Jesus must needs go through Samaria" (vs. 4). He had to go. It was necessary. But there was great enmity between Samaritans and the Jews. Why didn't he skirt the entire area? It would have been out of his way considerably to do so, but a stern legalistic Jew would travel miles out of his way to avoid an encounter with a Samaritan. But not Jesus! Long before the creation of the world, it had been settled in the counsels of eternity that Jesus was to meet a poor sinful Samaritan woman, and he could not forego that appointment.

I imagine that it still shocks the sensitivities of the legalists of our day when they come across this particular story in John's Gospel—somehow we'd rather disassociate Jesus from having anything to do with divorced people. But this woman was a divorcée many times over!

In the preceding chapter of John's Gospel, we see Jesus having an interview with Nicodemus, the respected religious leader of the Pharisees, a man who stood at the very top of the nation, likely one of the most prominent men of Jesus' day. In contrast, as Jesus came to the city of Sychar in Samaria, we observe him talking to a socially tainted woman of a scorned segregated race—one who has been described as a seeking, seductive, lonesome, passionate woman of dalliance, a castoff of five men and living unmarried with a sixth. It was high noon, more than likely a sweltering day. People stayed indoors to avoid the oppressive heat. But not this woman. She came to draw water at midday so as to avoid the contempt and scorn of the townspeople.

This woman was at the very bottom of the scrap heap of humanity. Apparently she had lost her faith and then, lacking any hold on God, in an effort to fill up the loneliness in her life and the void in her hungry heart, she made a shipwreck of her love life.

Jesus' approach to unsaved individuals was always shaped by his desire to save them. Everyone needs to be shown the way into the kingdom of God. What a person is on the outside is not important—it is what he can become on the inside after an encounter with the living Christ that matters most. A prolonged tete-a-tête over the top of a well not more than four feet across could constitute the basis for a public scandal. Jesus' conversation with this notorious woman affords us a beautiful view of the pure grace of God. Christ's discourse with the learned doctors of his day and his conversation with Moses and Elias on the mount are buried in silence in the Bible. How glad we can be, and thankful, that this conversation is preserved. We can read and listen while Jesus pours his deepest lesson; not for the mind, but this time a lesson about love, emotions, and gifts—his lesson for the heart into the heart of this woman. He saw in her a great need and opportunity, just as unique and important as his encounter with the respected Nicodemus.

Jesus was and is not concerned with the repulsive surface that covered and covers people's souls. He treated the woman with courtesy and kindness. He was gentle. He humbled himself and asked her for a drink of water. She recognized him as a Jew and with astonishment said, "How is it that Thou, being a Jew, askest drink of me, which am a woman of Samaria?" (vs. 9).

I get tears when I read that—I read between the lines, I'm afraid—I hear the pathetic note in her voice. She has been so scorned and left alone. Loneliness is heart-wrenching.

How graciously Jesus responded! He knows all men; he knew what she was; but he made the approach to her, not fearful of his reputation or what others might think or say. He was going to knock at the door of her heart. He was then and is today a seeking Savior.

Jesus felt the dryness of this woman's parched soul more than his own parched mouth. He was going to give her living water, and so in answer to her question he said, "If you only knew what a wonderful gift God has for you, and who I am, you would ask me for some *living* water!" (vs. 10).

Jesus knew that this woman could embrace this lesson. Gifts and love and divine grace are to be accepted, not necessarily understood. This woman knew much about giving. Five times she had given herself to a husband unreservedly, with pathetic results. The ardent husbands always ended up abandoning her. Sin had tripped her up badly through the years, resulting in distrust, cynicism, and hardness of heart. But she was a person, a personality, an individual with a great need. Jesus not only treated her kindly, but with equality. He genuinely esteemed her personality, making it easy for her to trust him and to identify with and accept him, thus stepping into the kingdom of God.

Jesus did not drive this woman away with threats, demeaning her, nor did he draw her with rewards. She was an outcast, floundering in repulsive sin, but she needed to be born again. Jesus could easily have alarmed and frightened her off at this point, but he quietly told her that people soon became thirsty again after drinking just water. "But the water

I give them," he said, "becomes a perpetual spring within them, watering them forever with eternal life" (vs. 13, 14).

The woman, listening intently, blurted out, "Please, sir, give me some of that water!" (vs. 15). Jesus' teaching at that moment was not fully understood; all she knew was that he was talking about something new and beautiful, something she'd been longing and searching for all her life. In Jesus' kind smile, his voice and manner, and in the loving look in his eyes, she saw the smile of a God who gives, loves, and forgives. What do divorced people see when they look into your eyes—condemnation or the love of God?

This woman knew that she didn't deserve what Jesus was offering—her past record and present low position rose up to convict her—but this troubled soul reached out for that which would satisfy her craving, her inner thirst. Who among us deserves God's grace? Is there anyone reading this who dares to stand up and state, "I deserve God's mercy"?

Very discreetly and kindly Jesus said, "Go and get your husband."

"But I'm not married," the woman replied.

"All too true!" Jesus said. "For you have had five husbands and you aren't even married to the man you're living with now."

"Sir," the woman said, "you must be a prophet." (vs. 16–19).

What a conversation! How we need to remember that Christ keeps an account of us all! He mildly told the woman that he knew all about her; but his reproof did not provoke. There is power in the Word of Christ when spoken as he speaks it. The woman was willing to continue the conversation. Jesus had not alienated himself from her by revealing what he knew.

The Master Physician opened the woman's wound of guilt, thus awakening her conscience so that she would be convinced of sin and appropriate the remedy of his grace and

51

love. The woman hungrily sought to receive more truth from him, and there was a lively discussion.

The revelation of her hidden life, the fact that Jesus dared to expose the whole sordid story, revealed such divine insight that she at once called him "a prophet" and began to question him regarding the place of worship. Her mistake lay in the fact that she thought of religion merely as a matter of form and ceremony. How many there are who make that tragic mistake!

Jesus continued talking to the woman at the well. He will always show himself to those who with an honest, humble heart desire to know him. Jesus said, "It's not *where* we worship that counts, but *how* we worship—is our worship spiritual and real? Do we have the Holy Spirit's help? For God is Spirit, and we must have His help to worship as we should. The Father wants this kind of worship from us" (vss. 23, 24).

There was recognition on the part of the woman that some mediator was necessary to give fuller knowledge of God. She got the message. "I know that the Messiah will come—the one they call Christ—and when He does, He will explain everything to us."

Then Jesus told her, "I am the Messiah!" (vss. 25, 26).

Did she believe? Her action was more eloquent than speech. I can just see her. Can you? When Jesus revealed his identity, I can picture her hands releasing their grip on her water pot, flying up to her face, and almost hear her gasp, "Messiah!" She repeats it to herself, looks once more into his tender eyes, notes the loving expression on his face, and turns running, leaving behind her water pot.

Jesus had a new disciple! A woman! A Samaritan woman at that, and one who had had five husbands!

I imagine that she ran all the way back to the village of Sychar—this woman who before would go to any means to avoid a confrontation with the townspeople. Her legs couldn't carry her fast enough. All the way I am certain she kept saying, "Messiah! Christ! The Messiah!" What joy there is when a sinner meets Jesus!

When she encountered the villagers, she told everyone, "Come and meet a man who told me everything I ever did!" (vs. 29).

One of the most remarkable things about this event occurred at this very point. Here was this woman of ill repute making this statement, actually admitting to her bad past; and the people dropped everything and listened. Not only did they listen, but the Bible says, "The people came streaming from the village to see Him" (vs. 30). It is incredible! Yet it happened.

Can Jesus use those who have failed so miserably in the past? Does past failure disqualify one for future usefulness? Can God bless the divorced individual? Does divorce mean career suicide for a Christian?

Notice the woman of Samaria at work for Jesus. The testimony of the many times married and divorced woman of Samaria resulted, the Bible says, in many believing he was the Messiah because of the woman's report and what they heard for themselves. Of him they said, "He is indeed the Savior of the world" (vs. 42b).

Someday we must all sit next to this woman and others like her if we are to enter our Father's kingdom. You may not like the idea of having to squeeze up to this "dirty little girl from Samaria"—or even of having to sit next to me or someone else who is divorced. But this is the way it is. The Bible declares, "For the Father seeketh such to worship Him" (vs. 23b).

In this encounter with the woman at the well and her subsequent transformation, we see God using a very weak and unlikely human instrument for the beginning of a great work among the Samaritans. She became his first massively persuasive evangelist, and the first to convey his mission beyond the bounds of his Jewish homeland. It was to a woman such as this that he chose to declare his universal messiahship. I am sure the disciples raised their eyebrows and wondered. Without question, Jesus completely disregarded the religious conventions of his day. This must have been hard to take for these followers of Jesus who were so steeped in Jewish law and tradition. Women were regarded mainly as chattels and breeders, to be subject to their male masters. The disciples were accustomed to hear the rabbis pray, "Blessed be thou for not having made me a Gentile or a woman"; so for Jesus to treat this woman as he did was nothing short of astounding!

In Jesus' example the disciples saw and learned. I wonder —can we today?

THINK ON THESE THINGS

Jesus did not alienate himself from the woman at the well by what he knew. He did not endorse her past sins; neither did he rebuke her for breaking God's law; but he gave her the Truth.

Jesus was love in action.

"Lord, when doubts fill my mind, when my heart is in turmoil, quiet me and give me renewed hope and cheer" (Ps. 94:19).

"Blessed be God who didn't turn away when I was praying, and didn't refuse me His kindness and love" (Ps. 66:20).

8
What about the Church and Divorce?

> The church can no longer ignore divorce nor can it afford to alienate the divorced individual—there are just too many of them around these days. Divorce is happening among too many Christian families. It's difficult to find a family anymore that hasn't been involved somewhere along the line in a divorce situation. And I don't look for it to get any better.

Those are the words of a Christian psychologist. He knows whereof he speaks. He is an authority in the field of family relations working, for the most part, with Christians.

In the process of working on this book we attended church one evening in a neighboring city with friends. They introduced us to a couple sitting in front of us. The name rang a bell, and I tapped the woman on the shoulder and said, "I know your daughter-in-law. We attended the same church as young girls many years ago." She turned, put her hand up to her head, and in an embarrassed whisper said, "She is no longer married to my son. There's been a divorce." Humiliation and hurt were written all over her kind face. I leaned close to her, patted her shoulder gently, and assured her I understood as I shared with her.

I find it alarming and disturbing as I note the trend. It is a tragic commentary on what is happening to the time-honored institution of marriage, even among Christians. What do the statistics reveal? Actually statistics are easily misinterpreted and often misleading. They are also conflicting. According to the magazine *Applied Christianity*, May, 1974, nearly two old marital unions are being terminated in the courts for every five new ones contracted at the altar. This is statistical information gleaned from the National Center for Health Statistics in Washington, D.C.

In its latest report on births, marriages, divorces, and deaths, the center noted that there were 1,727,000 marriages in the United States and 678,000 divorces. This is a ratio of one divorce for each 2.56 marriages.

At the time of this writing, marriages and divorce are both up over 1973 statistics, but the increase in divorces is much greater than that in marriages.

The national divorce rate, expressed in number of divorces per year per 1,000 population, is continuing a long, steady rise, the report reveals. The rate was 3.4 in 1970, 3.6 in 1971, 4.0 in 1972, and 4.3 in 1973.

In talking to many individuals, I find there is a great deal of ignorance about the churches' views regarding divorce. It is generally believed that the Catholic church is strongly opposed to divorce. This is true, but what is less generally known and understood is that the Protestant church, comprising a vast number of denominations, has equally strong views on the subject of divorce. This comes as a surprise, if not a shock, to many who are generally considered to be outside the ranks of evangelical, conservative, fundamental Protestantism.

There is a tremendous depth of struggle going on in both the Catholic and Protestant church as it relates to divorced persons. Churchmen in Rome, for instance, have been meeting for years to debate new divorce referendums. The divorce question strikes deep chords in Italian life that affects Roman Catholics around the world. It is stated that logical, legal arguments are blurred by emotional and sociological overtones.[1]

Italy was the twenty-seventh nation with a Roman

Catholic majority to introduce divorce. Only the European countries of Spain, Ireland, Malta, and Andorra have no divorce. One Italian career woman, divorced, says, "Divorce is still considered by most Italians to be a form of alienation, a stigma. Even though many Italian spouses do violate the conventions of marriage, they still consider the institution itself to be inviolate."[2]

The Catholic church, it cannot be disputed, has done an effective job in instilling into the minds of her people that divorce is godless and out of the question. What is overlooked, however, is the fact that at the time the Italian divorce law was passed (December 1, 1970), there were an estimated five million so-called "outlaws of matrimony," that is, men and women and their offspring who were bound together in stable yet irregular and legally unrecognized unions. And what is also overlooked is the fact that many couples are living in a virtual state of war and undivorce, with husbands having mistresses and wives having lovers. This is true not only among Catholics, but also Protestants. By many who live this way, this is regarded as the lesser of two evils.

How many there are within the church who are merely keeping up an image or front cannot be known. A divorce would shatter this image and false front. It also might very well mean the loss of one's job and position and standing in the eyes of the Christian world. Whether we like labels or not, in simple terms it is living a lie. Many churchmen prefer, however, to label it keeping the home together. The sin of infidelity may not be winked at, but at least it's tolerated in favor of avoiding a divorce.

Bernard Ramm, a well-known Protestant theologian, makes this observation:

> To maintain a destructive marriage on the basis of being loyal to a Christian ethic of no divorce is hardly justifiable. Love, justice, mercy, and redemption are

ground underfoot to preserve a moralistic view. If a pastor does not believe in divorce, in many of these cases he should at least be ready to advise separation of bed and board.

Each case has to be settled in terms of its own configuration of factors. There is little that rules can do in such unique situations. The only rule is really the rule of redemption: the church ought to follow ethical policies that are redemptive, that are healing, that offer hope for happiness in the future, and that do not intend to harm or hurt people simply to comply with the ethics of their "in group."[3]

A Catholic, vehemently opposed to divorce, passionately declared: "Why am I against divorce? Because divorce denies love. I find adultery, and even wife-murder, better than divorce, because they are more in keeping with love."[4]

One gasps at such reasoning. But I also gasped one day while listening to a radio talk-show interview. The interviewer was talking to a lady who had just observed her fiftieth wedding anniversary. He congratulated her and then asked if she'd ever considered divorce during all those years. Her answer was a loud and definite "No!" It was said with distaste and scorn. "Divorce? Absolutely not," she emphasized. "But murder? You'll never know how many times I've wanted to kill my husband!" It was said with deadly earnestness; she wasn't laughing. When asked why she was so opposed to divorce, the woman replied, "Because the church is against it." I wished I could have been the interviewer. I would like to have asked the dear woman if she didn't think the church was against murder. Didn't she know one of the Ten Commandments is "Thou shalt not kill"?

Oh, but you say, those are exaggerations. No one would say that adultery and wife- or husband-murder are better than divorce. One wonders. What I report to you is the truth as I have heard it and read it.

I think of the woman who wrote a letter to a Christian organization asking to have her name removed from their mailing list. The letter stated, "I've been on your mailing list ever since you began, but since I know your new editor is divorced, I don't want anything to do with you." Never mind the fact that thousands of lives were being reached and touched by the writing and editing of that editor; never mind the fact that the woman's own children were victims of marital difficulties and divorce, or that her husband died of the long-range effects of overindulgence in alcoholic beverages (one could stop and ask why). Did the Christian organization comply with the request that if the editor was removed the woman might reconsider and continue her support? The editor's name was removed, though the editor stayed on. Some kind of a good compromise, you say? What the woman writing the letter didn't know was that behind the scenes in that organization there were other divorced people—godly, dedicated individuals who had been there for years, who handled her letters, her financial gifts, and even saw to it that she received her paper regularly.

Other instances could be given. There is no need; nor do I wish to infer with a blanket statement that all churches and all Christians and Christian organizations regard divorce with such rigidity or treat the divorced person with such contempt. Thank God for churches and Christian organizations that recognize the needs and the worth of one human soul, the God-given gifts and potential in every individual regardless of one's marital standing. I know of scores of such churches and Christian groups, and so do you.

One divorced individual said, however:

> I get the eerie feeling that I'm some sort of hideous person, but then I look in the mirror and know I look better than I've ever looked in my life. I feel healthier—mentally and physically—than I ever did when I had ulcers, colitis, you name it, anything that

had to do with nerves. Please tell your readers I've been able to throw away all my bottles of tranquilizers and prescription drugs since the divorce. Who needs them when you're finally living at peace! There are times, though, when I really hurt as I see the Christian world coming down on divorce like a herd of elephants, always pointing it out as being so sinful. What's so righteous about a marriage when all the couple does is argue and fight?

It is a known fact that many churches do not allow the divorced individual to serve on their church boards as deacons, elders, or in other leadership positions such as teaching Sunday school, and so on. Said one such ostracized individual, "This is one of the cruelest things being done to divorced people. Some of us are talented and would like to continue to exercise our God-given gifts."

Another astute Christian said, "The sin of divorce—when forgiven by God—should not rule one out of a position of church service any more than the sin of drunkenness or gossip—when they are forgiven by God."[5]

It is heartening to hear people like Dr. Bernard L. Ramm come out and say that in the broader Christian ethic about divorce, attempts need to be made to solve "some of these wretchedly complex cases by a spirit of love, of understanding, and of redemption. Such an ethic attempts to work the best it can within Christian presuppositions of knowledge about divorce gained from sociologists, psychologists, doctors, and lawyers. The attempt is to salvage or redeem life rather than to treat people in a strict, moralistic, and legalistic manner."[6]

In May, 1970, writer James Johnson struck a tender spot among many Christians and in many churches by asking the question, "Divorced Persons: Do They Have a Place in Your Church?" It was an article appearing in *Christian Life* magazine. His incisive writing often smacks where it hurts the most. Sometimes there is a barb in his pen that catches and irritates, but it is done with loving concern designed to make the reader sit up, take notice, and move into action. Johnson writes that the church has a responsibility to bring reconciliation in all cases where a home is breaking up; but where there is nothing left to reconcile, what then?

He goes on to ask, "Can the church condescend to open her arms to lives broken by a failing marriage, regardless of the circumstances? Is it possible that the church could heal these people by love and mercy?" He cites the illustration of a woman who moved to another community and to another church—"far less orthodox unfortunately," he states—where she is now experiencing something of God's healing.

> There may be some relief in her former church now that a "sticky problem" has been removed. But who picks up the tab for the life that was bent in the process?
>
> Have we followed Jesus' example? He faced up to the law regarding adultery and told the woman taken in the very act, "Neither do I condemn thee; go and sin no more."

Johnson concludes his article with these thought-provoking words:

> It seems we've got a long way to go yet to reach His standard.[7]

What exactly was Jesus' standard in regard to that incident? It would appear that the Master was saying that throwing stones is mighty risky business! Jesus was showing that it is not uncommon for those who are indulgent in their own sin to be severe against the sins of others. It was true that Moses in the law commanded that such as this woman taken in adultery were to be stoned to death. The Pharisees in dragging this woman before Jesus were trying to trip him up. (A seemingly favorite pastime of theirs, not too out of date today in some Christian circles. Couldn't they find anything better to do with their time?) But Jesus skillfully avoided the snare which they had laid for him. He neither reflected upon the law, nor did he, on the other hand, encourage them to stone her. He appealed, by his actions and the few words he did speak, to those who were condemning her as to whether they were fit to be her prosecutors. Did they dare take away a life with their hands which they were already taking away with their tongues? Would their own consciences fly in their faces if they did? (Aren't you glad others around you can't see your conscience?)

Jesus stooped down and wrote in the dust with his finger. They kept demanding an answer, so he stood up again and said, "All right, hurl the stones at her until she dies. But only he who never sinned may throw the first!" Then he stooped down again and wrote some more in the dust. The Jewish leaders slipped away one by one, beginning with the eldest, until only Jesus was left in front of the crowd with the woman. Then Jesus stood up again and said to her, "Where are your accusers? Didn't even one of them condemn you?"

"No, sir," she said.

And Jesus said, "Neither do I. Go and sin no more" (John 8:6b–11).

Jesus was building upon an uncontested maxim in morality: that it is very absurd for any of us to be zealous in seeing to it that the offenses of others are punished while we are every bit as guilty ourselves—if not in regard to that particular offense, then surely in some other manner; and if not in actual deed, then in thought. Sin is sin in God's eyes. Who are we—mere men—to place labels on whose sin is more ugly, or which sin is the worst? We stand self-condemned when we judge others without first recognizing our own guilt and sin. Jesus is teaching that we must love the sinner while hating the sin. Always we must remember our own corrupt nature. There is an old maxim which says, "We either are, or have been, or may be, what he [or she] is."

Surely remembering this should restrain us from throwing stones at anyone.

Jesus always aimed to bring the sinner to repentance, but in this instance he also wanted her would-be prosecutors to see their own sin. Jesus came to seek and to save, not to destroy. Isn't that still supposed to be the mission of the church today?

> As Christians, we must forever reject the Pharisaical approach toward those who are divorced. Ostracizing those who are divorced is most unchristian. Throwing stones at particular sins is unrewarding and self-deceiving. Jesus reminded a group of Pharisees of that when He said, "Let him who is without sin cast the first stone." It is our ministry to create a feeling of fellowship and understanding for anyone who has sinned and is seeking God's forgiveness. We should remember that the church is a rehabilitation center for all of us, not a sorority for sophisticated sinners.[8]

> Jesus' action is a potent protest against legalism. If He had been a legalist, since He was without sin He Himself was duty bound to throw the stones. But He was not a legalist. He explicitly told her He was not condemning her. From now on she was to be no longer sinning. She was to come to know God's will and conform her life to that will. Jesus' action is a warning to us.[9]

Today God is not writing men's sins in the sand, as it is believed that Jesus was doing that day; but the Bible teaches in many places that a record is being kept, written as with a pen of iron and the point of a diamond (Jer. 17:1), never to be forgotten till they are forgiven. Happy are we if we have no reason to be afraid of Christ's writing!

I think there is a lesson here, too, for those of us who are divorced. One of the things each of us battles—and I have heard it from everyone with whom I have talked, and I have already alluded to it in a previous chapter—is this thing of bitterness. We do feel maligned, judged, talked about, and sometimes even hated. But if we hope to be forgiven by our Judge—God himself—then we must forgive our accusers; we must not be guilty of judging those who would throw stones. Let our own witness be true.

When Jesus said, "I do not condemn thee," he was, in effect, saying, "I do forgive thee." He knows the hardness of all our hearts; yet he also sees our tender insides and knows the longing within. It seems a paradox: can we be both hard and tender at the same time?

It is even as Jesus said, that it was because of the hardness of men's hearts that Moses allowed divorce (Matt. 19:8). But Christians are to live under the liberty of love and display a tenderness of heart, forbearing one another, forgiving one another, in love. The hardness of our hearts—the inability to hurdle whatever it was that contributed to and caused divorce—need not spoil the rest of our life and our relationship to Christ and others. Jesus' words to the woman that day were, "Go and sin no more." Christ's favor to her and to us—all of us who name his name—is a strong argument to put aside our rebellions and differences, whatever it is that stands in the way of a right relationship to him and with others, and to go on living for him, sinning no more. When we sin, we should remember we have an advocate, Jesus Christ. He is faithful when we confess and turn to him.

In all our dealings with those who are divorced, we must recognize a certain defensiveness on their part. Rather than criticize them for it, or fault them for such an attitude, which may show forth in some bitterness at times, may I suggest that you can help them by realistically trying to fit yourself into their shoes. There is a terribly "alone" feeling which sets in. One divorcée explained it like this: "I feel neither fish nor fowl. I'm not married, and I'm not really single. I don't belong with the married church people anymore—I'm regarded by some now as a threat—and I certainly don't belong with the singles." It is a dilemma peculiar to the divorced individual.

I appreciated so much what Thomas H. Cosgrove wrote in an article entitled "What Divorced Catholics Need Most."[10] He says:

> It is generally agreed that in our Catholic parishes we fall short of ideal Christian community. I can recall frequent interviews in rectories with persons who began by saying, "I am divorced." And then pausing, as if waiting to be banished. When some rapport was established, they would say, "It is the way people look at me that makes me withdraw."

Cosgrove goes on to say:

> He [the divorced person] has reconciled himself to an extraordinary life, but he finds himself less at home with old friends. He wonders if he is suspected of looking for a new wife in his friends' homes. He may be reluctant to be usher, or lector, since he feels that, somehow, the fabric of Christianity is soiled in the sight of others.
>
> Divorced people are especially prone to shun old friends for fear of being regarded as a threat to a happy marriage. It is the very person who is least likely to want to hurt another person's life who will pull himself away from the parish and the homes in the parish he once frequented. Surely the most imperfect Catholic community should be able to lovingly say the warm word, and give the look, not of disdain nor of indifference, but the look of love to the divorced of the household of the faith.
>
> The divorced of whom I speak, and there are many of them, do not want or expect your daily reassurance, a

room in your house, your spouse as helpmate, your children as surrogate offspring. They do desire, especially those who do not overtly seek it, the look of love built of the same beauty that Christ gave to St. Peter.

As a Christian, you are gifted by the Holy Spirit to give this reassurance, sometimes by word, deed, or the simple but eloquent look. Christ is already looking at these men and women in this way, but barring a miracle or extraordinary faith, they need also a word from human lips and a glance from human eyes which, while not sufficient to remove all scars, may be enough to reveal to them their inherent nobility. The divorced I speak of are not greedy. They do not expect a largess of the good things of life, but they hope for the sign that looks upon them and sees that they are good.

Ernst Larson expressed this well in the title of his book. . . . He gathered, it seems to me, the look Christ gave to Peter, and the look we owe to our divorced friends, who seem to be fading from the human scene, in the relevant words: *Hey! I Love You, Is That Okay?* Some of your divorced friends are waiting for you to say this, or show it with your eyes.

But what can the church, therefore, do for those who are divorced, and for the children of divorce? It is always an encouraging sign to read articles urging the church to face the divorce problem realistically. Writer Catharine Brandt in an article entitled "Facing Divorce"[11] admits that the theological aspects of divorce are great, but she strongly urges that the church also look at the practical aspects of the problem. There is a need for some kind of realistic balance.

The Sunday school can be a very stabilizing influence. She says:

The Sunday School has a grave responsibility to teach Biblical precepts, but it also has an opportunity to show love and compassion to its members (and their children) who find themselves in unfortunate circumstances.

What is your Sunday School doing for the couple whose marriage is fractured? For the family whose father has left them? For the divorcée who "sticks it out" in the church in the face of disapproval? If the Sunday School helps even one such family get its footing again, such efforts are worthwhile.

Writer Brandt cites the divorcée who says the day her divorce was granted was the loneliest day of her life. "Where was the church?" the divorcée asked. "I had taught Sunday School for a dozen years, but not one teacher called me."

The article relates what happened to a woman named Sylvia who taught a class of junior high age. Although the heartache and bitter experiences that led to her divorce may have prepared her to be even a better teacher, equipped to warn her junior high pupils of the pitfalls ahead, she was relieved of her teaching position the day she got her divorce. Sad to say, heartless treatment caused her to leave the church she had served for years. No one knows the amount of harm done.

On the positive side, which also exists among many churches who open their arms to divorced individuals, the same article relates how a small church in Minnesota welcomed a divorced mother and her three children. After a conversion experience, the woman was allowed to teach Sunday school until her death. One of her sons went to Bible school, assisted by church members. He became a missionary and is now the pastor of a large church. The other children are also Christians and working in their Sunday schools.

The same article states:

> In another church a young couple with compassion and children of the same ages as those of a young divorcée determined to show their Christian concern and love.

They invited Marlene and her children to their home for dinner once a month, on Saturdays. "It's been a workout, a hectic day, with all those kids together, but I feel we've helped Marlene a small bit. Russ takes her boys to ball games. Just sharing a dad has helped the boys to overcome feelings of rejection."

The mother of a young woman undergoing divorce proceedings called the girl's former Sunday School teacher.

"Please pray for Bev. This is the day her divorce becomes final."

Surprised and aghast, the teacher thought, It's a little late to pray for Bev now that the story is over. Then she remembered a poster that hung in her daughter's room: Today is the first day of the rest of your life.

Of course, she thought, the past is behind Bev. She has the rest of her life ahead of her. What can I do to help Bev face the future? She spent a long time on her knees praying for both herself—her attitudes—and Bev. Then she wrote the girl a note inviting her to spend the next Sunday with her.

A young divorcée and her children were lost to one church simply because no one thought to pick them up for class. After her divorce the young woman had no car.[12]

One woman told me of a most heartbreaking situation which occurred in her situation as it related to the Sunday school. I repeat it only to caution churches against allowing this type of thing to occur if they can possibly help it. Debby stated:

I was the one secure thing left to my son. But he was almost destroyed by his Sunday School teacher, who was giving him his interpretation of the Bible's teachings on divorce. It was tearing my son apart. When I discovered what was happening after questioning my son and finally getting him to tell me, I went to the minister about it, and he put a stop to it. The minister and church officers were terribly sorry it happened. If I hadn't been a member of the church and known the pastor well enough to feel free to talk to him, I would never have stepped inside that church again, nor allowed my children back in that Sunday School.

That same church has shown a truly beautiful and remarkable spirit in welcoming into its midst as an assistant pastor a divorced man. His own testimony concerning the chaotic struggle he went through, and his subsequent healing as a result of the love and acceptance shown by his former church and now this present church are illustrative of the kind of compassion and understanding that Jesus himself showed. He says, "I never stand in the pulpit without a tremendous awareness that apart from the grace of God and his forgiveness in my life, I would be a wretched human being." You can be sure that such an awareness shows in this pastor's total ministry.

I contrast that to a former neighbor who was a missionary. Her marriage was a disaster and, after four years, she could no longer endure the hypocrisy and secured a divorce, returning to the States. Her alienation from the church was complete and to date has not been restored. That happened in 1960. Today I believe she would stand a better chance of being accepted by the same church denomination. But it is a great tragedy, affecting not only her but two sons as well. She refuses to discuss the subject, recalling what happened years ago as being "too painful." Such as these, however, must recognize that they are accountable to God for their own souls, even though others may have contributed to antagonizing them against the church. We do not look at people who are fallible and who can fail us, but we keep our eyes on Jesus, who is faithful. It is God who will judge us someday righteously if we do not accept his forgiveness, love, and mercy now. And there is forgiveness and understanding from him.

Another divorcée tells of her daughter dropping out of youth activities at the church because the young people and their leader embarrassed her by constantly praying about her parents' divorce and asking God to effect a reconciliation. When the divorce was finally granted, she felt so alien to her friends and what she called "their funny attitude" that she refused to attend any more meetings. Perhaps the feelings were more on the part of the teen-age daughter than the members of the youth group, but it was unfortunate and might have been prevented with a little more discernment regarding the practical aspects of that particular family situation, a realistic understanding that the girl's parents wouldn't be getting a divorce if the one instigating it didn't feel it was necessary, and more sensitivity on the part of the youth leaders.

Many churches do have successful adult singles groups which encourage and attract the divorced person. In such churches there are (where the church is large enough) groups for both younger and older singles. It is not unusual for happy remarriages to spring forth from such groups, though that should not be the sole reason the divorced individual attends. These groups have dynamic Bible studies, interesting social times, and lively discussions. More and more churches are finding it necessary to have such groups to meet the needs of their people. In many other churches, however, the divorced individual is the forgotten Christian.

But in talking with most pastors, I found a great loving concern for the divorced persons to whom they minister. One pastor shared that when he first came to the church 65 percent of the people were divorced. Another pastor said 35 percent of his people were divorced; still another said 50 percent. It is a spiraling figure in most churches. In southern California, where I live and where the research for this book was done, it was not difficult to find churches whose pastors were divorced. In every instance I found dynamic, growing ministries, and the church was forward-looking and moving spiritually.

The early church held to the view that marriage must be viewed as a permanent, binding, lifelong commitment. Throughout the Christian tradition, this has been upheld as a basic principle. My own Protestant background clung tenaciously to the belief that divorce was a no-no, the thought not even to be entertained for one moment. I can remember the whispered rumors and comments when I was a child in our small Iowa community and a divorced woman came to live in our town. (She didn't remain long.) One of my cousins was a divorcée and regarded with great suspicion even among her relatives. Yet in that small Dutch community there was a greater preponderance of hasty have-to marriages than any other place I have ever heard about. (Immorality can be tolerated with beautiful church weddings, but the divorced person is an embarrassment to the same church.)

In view, however, of the undeniable fact that the divorce rate is phenomenally high and increasing, the church is being forced to rethink its position and adjust to the realities of the present social and cultural situation. By some this is regarded as capitulation and compromise. Others regard it as flexibility and realism. I personally am led to believe that Jesus would seek out divorced people, go to their homes, converse warmly with them, and invite them to be a part of the local church. I can testify to the fact that this was done by several pastors in communities where I have lived in recent years and where I have visited churches and signed visitor's cards. The warmth and love extended meant more to me than I can possibly convey in a book such as this. There is a book on my bookshelf with the intriguing title, *Helping Each Other Be Human*,[13] and that really is the name of the game. In this game called life we all need all the help we can get, never deny it. And the church is one of the unique means God has so ordained whereby his love and help can be dispersed to a needy world.

I believe David R. Mace sums this up most admirably when he says that the individual pastor, wherever he personally stands regarding the church's attitude to divorce, must make the utmost effort of which he is capable to provide help to men and women in his community who are involved in the breakdown of their marriages. There can be no possible question regarding the pastor's duty here. Wherever there is human need, he is pledged to do what lies in his power to meet it. Condemnation or judgment of the divorced person, or self-righteous aloofness from his distress, are unpardonable from a humane, let alone a Christian, point of view. In most instances, divorcing and divorced persons are the unhappy victims of our corporate blindness, stupidity, and neglect. They deserve and need both sympathy and succor. The great majority of them marry again; and if we deplore the fact that their first marriage failed, this should imbue us with zealous determination to enable them to ensure the success of their second attempt.

No policy or program the church may devise can be effective unless it is based on an accurate and sympathetic comprehension of the need of those people for whom divorce is not a theoretical concept, but a grim and practical reality.[14]

What about the church and divorce? Of course it must take a firm stand upholding God's ideal, God's standard of marriage and divorce, just as it does other teachings of the Bible.

> But the ministries of the pastor and the church (the church's people) should be available for divorced people. Christ died for them. They need the Lord and the church. The church (Christians) should not shun, condemn, or humiliate them, but rather seek to win

them to Christ and to build them up in Christian character and usefulness.[15]

The church can never condone divorce or the things which produce it. The divorced man and woman would be remiss to expect this, and the church would be wrong to practice it.[16]

There is only one answer to the question, "What about the church and divorce?" It is the practice of Christian love. In our church services we frequently sing the old Gospel songs which say, "Christ receiveth sinful men," and such words as "There's room at the cross for you." Do we mean it when we sing it?

THINK ON THESE THINGS

A Christian pastor made this observation:

The last thing you should be in the Christian world is a divorced person. You will be welcome and accepted— even receive "star billing" and may appear on the platform with the "religious greats" if you are a former murderer, drug addict, member of a subversive organization, or guilty at one time of some notorious crime—but did you ever see a divorced Christian recognized as being divorced?

These things also belong to the wise. It is not good to have respect of persons in judgment (Prov. 24:23, *AV*).

Peter opened his mouth, and said, "Of a truth I perceive that God is no respector of persons: But in every nation he that feareth him, and worketh righteousness, is accepted with him" (Acts 10:34, *AV*).

9
What about the Children of Divorce?

"What were you trying to prove? So what good is a martyred mother?" A friend was questioning my motives for keeping the marriage together when the situation within our home had been tense and difficult for many years. I had replied that we kept the marriage together "mainly for the sake of the children."

That is the number one reason many couples give for sticking it out as long as they do. They are living in what I have referred to before as a state of undivorce—legally married, but emotionally divorced. What they fail to realize is that the emotional climate created within the home by such an arrangement makes for an extremely unhealthy environment for everyone concerned, in particular the growing child. I am grateful to Dr. Bernard Ramm for confirming from a theologian's point of view what many psychologists and child counselors have been saying for years. He states, "It is common knowledge with psychologists that a bad marriage is psychologically destructive. It creates bitter, hostile, and unforgiving attitudes in the couple. It may work all sorts of psychological damage on the children."[1]

Dr. J. Louise Despert, child psychiatrist and author of the book *Children of Divorce*, writes:

> It is not divorce, but the emotional situation in the home, with or without the divorce, that is the deter-

mining factor in the child's adjustment. A child is very disturbed when the relationship between his parents is very disturbed. . . . Divorce (in these circumstances) is not automatically a destructive experience. It may also be a cleansing and healing one, for the child as well as you. Divorce is not the costliest experience for a child. Unhappy marriage without divorce . . . can be far more destructive.[2]

While we are so prone to point out the damaging effects we believe are incurred as a result of divorce upon our children—who are often referred to as "the innocent victims of divorce"—very little is said to point up what happens to children who are forced to grow up in loveless, friction-ridden, supposedly happy homes. In our anxiety to preserve the externals we sacrifice our children, who, as a result, may go through life bearing permanent emotional scars. It has been shown time after time by counselors and professionals dealing with couples having conflict in their marriages, that many hangups and problems of one or both partners in the marriage can be traced directly to their growing up years within the home.

Letters to the editors of newspapers, to Ann Landers, Dear Abby, and other such columns can be very revealing. Frequently you will find letters such as this:

We have been married for fifteen years, which can be described as miserable to say the least. Three of our four children are in school and have nervous problems, which have been diagnosed as emotional immaturity. The fourth child isn't in school yet.

I know divorce is sin and have prayed for a solution. Meanwhile I am staying with my husband until the children are raised, but increasingly I am coming to believe that they are being affected very adversely by the marriage anyway. Why doesn't God answer my prayers? What should I do about the marriage? Will this cause emotional problems in my children? Please answer as soon as possible. (Signed) Deeply Troubled.

The editor's letter stated that saving a marriage for children when the situation is like this is a poor reason, since parents cannot hide intense feelings toward each other from their children. Such negativism toward each other produces a very unhealthy emotional environment for children.

The answer further stated the editor's belief that God does not give us answers to prayers when there are some decisions and actions we alone can take, based on the situation at hand and what appears to be the reasonable, logical, right alternative for the best welfare of everyone concerned. "God does not give us guidance unless we are willing to make decisions. No one else can make the decision regarding divorce for you, and you alone are responsible for the results."

Another letter in the newspaper told of a wife's plight. She stated she felt like a robot who was wound up every morning and programmed to do whatever her husband wanted her to do. The wife said her husband was not much of a father to their three children, but that he devoted most of his time to his business or other people. All she received from her husband was lectures. This frustrated woman stated that she wanted "out of this jail I'm living in. If it weren't for the kids I'd have left him long ago. How important is it for children to have a father?" She signed her letter "Going Nuts."

The reply to this woman said, "You can't be staying in that jail because you don't want to deprive your children of a father. From what you say, he's not much of a father anyway. Children need at least one sane parent."

It is the privilege and responsibility of parents to guide their children in ways that will insure healthy adulthood. Could it be that the great number of divorces we are seeing all across the land are the result of individuals who have not seen beautiful love relationships within their homes as they were growing up simply because their parents were merely tolerating each other "for the sake of the children"? Could it be that the increasing number of divorces, even among Christians, is a recognition on the part now of those who seek to be honest with the Lord, themselves, their children, and others, that they cannot go on living a lie—that it will, in fact, have adverse effects upon their children?

Citing Dr. Ramm again, he asks the question, "What does this inflation of divorces mean?" and answers it by stating: "To some it is a sign of a decadent civilization. To others it is a sign that our present marriage system is no longer relevant to modern society and some new pattern is in the making. To others it is a sign that people are now more honest. When they realize that a marriage is a mistake, they do not senselessly continue it creating more psychological damage all the way around."[3]

How can children learn to have beautiful, meaningful love relationships with members of the opposite sex if they do not see such love practices within their home as they are growing up? Some conflict within marriage and within the home is natural, but when it is persistent, when there is tension, discord and a constant feeling of disharmony, children cannot help but be affected.

Of course children are hurt when they see their parents being hostile and indifferent to each other; of course they are going to be confused and disillusioned when they see no outward demonstrations of thoughtfulness, kindness, and love between mother and father. Where do children learn such values? It is one thing to read to them from the Bible about being kind, tenderhearted, and kindly affectioned, but for these virtues to ring true, they must see them in action. Yes, within the home.

How flat the words of 1 Corinthians 13 sound when you

read them aloud to your children and such love is not practiced with your mate! How distasteful Ephesians 5 is when it speaks of the relationship between husbands and wives, and you know that your children know you are not living up to that ideal!

How can children learn to have beautiful, meaningful love that love is beautiful, that marriage is a sacred thing to be cherished, valued, and sacrificed for; that it can be joyful—when year after year they are seeing something so sub-ideal? What a distortion of truth! To focus on preserving the outward form of marriage while doing nothing to improve the content is a farce that is perpetuated in many families, including Christian homes.

What do we mean when we say we are staying married "for the sake of our children"? Are we not making martyrs of ourselves? And what does it really prove? If it means we are being obedient to what God says about divorce, what does this do to our obedience in regard to other aspects of living—truthfulness, thoughtfulness, respect, and love itself?

When my friend accused me of playing the role of a martyred mother, I did not appreciate the insinuation; in fact, it upset me more than just a little. Tears were shed as I denied any such thing—hadn't I done the right and honorable thing? But slowly the truth began to surface as I faced my inner thoughts. How many times had I taken out my resentments on my children, feeling as I did that I was making a great sacrifice for them! Often I wanted to hurry their childhood along, to get through the long, sad days, hoping to reach some better tomorrow. My unspoken attitude must have been absorbed by the children. Children are so keenly sensitive, and I now realize that ours were especially so. Many times the two oldest children would catch me crying silently or sitting alone in the big chair in the living room in the dark enveloped by despair. My tense, unhappy face must have reflected my inner anguish. What anxiety and confusion this must have caused in their childish hearts!

Is it fair to children to burden them with the feeling that they were responsible for keeping their parents together and depriving them of years that they might have been using to rebuild their lives and find a measure of happiness? It is a debt children do not deserve, nor is it one they can ever repay. It is a sacrifice, however, which you and you alone can make. The value and gains must be carefully weighed against any feelings of resentment that may crop up later, both on your part and on the part of your children. I have heard divorced individuals say, "Why did I do it? My kids didn't appreciate it at the time, and they sure don't think any better of me for it now."

What about the children of divorce? What does divorce do to them? There can be no pat answer. What happens to the children of divorce in one situation may not effect the children of divorce in another home at all. The effect can be totally different. It has been rightly pointed out that there is no typical child of a shattered home, no typical reaction, no typical kind of hurt among children victimized by unstable, crumbling homes. But there are patterns. Invariably, children are caught in the middle of the agony of a breaking home. Mothers and fathers use them, often, as levers against each other. And for nearly all children there is a pattern of instability, loneliness, guilt, and feelings of responsibility of the kind that only children are capable of feeling.

There can be no question about it, divorce is a major crisis for the children of divorce and for their parents. The most important thing parents can do for their children in the crisis days immediately surrounding the divorce proceedings is to give their children the reassurance that they are deeply loved, and that they will be taken care of. They need also the assurance that they are not responsible for the divorce and that they will still be seeing both parents. When divorce hits a family, the children need to know that they are not being divorced from their parents' affections, and that they are not being abandoned.

Our children did not ask to be born. We have no right, therefore, to handicap them for life by inflicting our problems upon them. I firmly believe that children of divorce can come out of the situation as more understanding, capable, loving human beings if the parents are willing to work at helping them. Children will be able to accept the situation with the same degree of composure or lack of it that we exhibit. It is possible to level with one's children, teaching them that suffering is a part of living but that we are able to surmount our difficulties through the strength and enabling which God provides. Even though we may fail in human relationships, God is unfailing. The Bible can become meaningful in an even more vital way as we relate biblical truth and then discuss how this can become practicable in our own experience.

The greater responsibility for this is thrust upon the mother in most instances, as she is usually the one who retains custody of the children. But the former spouse can assist in his way whenever he has the children.

Many of the women divorcées whom I interviewed told me that they felt their children had established a far better relationship with their father after the divorce than they ever had within the conflict of keeping the home together. They said their children saw more of their father now than while they were married. And that the times when the children were with their father was quality time, if not always quantity. One married son said to me, "My dad takes my younger brother places he never took me. He does things with Jimmy that he never did with me. Jimmy is developing a much better relationship with Dad than I ever had or will have. . . . I have too many bitter memories."

The success of this, however, depends upon the woman's ability to keep from degrading her former mate, the father of her children. The very worst thing a woman can do for her children if she divorces their father is to denigrate him in their eyes. She owes it to them and to her former husband to allow him to establish a relationship with them, and for the children to love and accept him because he is their father. By the same token a man owes this to his former wife, the mother of his children. Be certain you do nothing to encourage hostility. How unjust it is and cruel to use the children as pawns or to exploit them. Do not vent your anger toward your former mate on your child or take out your unhappiness on the child. Nothing is accomplished by vindictiveness. I have always told our children that you earn a much better response (in all of life's situations) by love.

I have never tried to alienate the children from their father. He is a good father, and worthy of their love and respect. I have, rather, urged them to be doubly kind and considerate, and to spend as much time with him as possible. Where there have been close family ties, children of divorce should not be denied the benefit of such warm and loving relationships. Children need the special kind of love that comes from grandparents, aunts, uncles, and cousins. If some bitterness exists, it is the better part of wisdom for this to be discussed between former in-laws and yourself. In an atmosphere of calmness, speak to each other about the necessity to refrain from making inflammatory and derogatory remarks that can only hurt and harm the children. Avoid being bitter and uncommunicative. It helps always to remember that the Bible cautions against this.

It is a serious mistake to shield children of divorce from the truth. They must be helped to face the reality of the situation and the finality of it. It is unbelievably cruel to lead them along or to give them false hope when you know it does not exist. Neither should you evade answering their questions.

Children must be told the truth. . . . It is far more intelligent to say "We made a mistake when we married and we are now going to live apart. We will do our best to love and care for you in spite of our problems with one another" than to invent a monstrous lie. Mystery will make children anxious; lies will make them distrustful.[4]

It is generally believed that children from divorced homes are less likely to have strong religious ties and are more willing to enter into interfaith marriages. But this need not be the case for children from divorced homes where the parents do maintain that they are Christians. In the Old Testament, God commands the Israelites to make known his word to their children and to their children's children, that they might not be as their fathers, a stubborn and rebellious generation (Ps. 78:4–8). This is amplified in the New Testament with the command that parents bring up their children in the nurture and admonition of the Lord.

I am sure most divorced Christians cringe when they read or hear about rebellious children and the comment is made, "They come from a broken home." When I read that the generation gap, the delinquent youngster, the divorce court, and the domestic strain and drain are current phrases to sum up today's family problems, I feel a great responsibility to make certain our failure in marriage does not adversely affect our children. Perhaps a greater awareness such as this on the part of more divorced parents can help to overcome this threat as we consciously work with our children. It hurts very much to hear a minister expound from the pulpit or see a writer go into great detail about this in some magazine article, and to have the implication made that all children of divorce go down the divorce drain with their delinquent parents. I trust this book will help people to see the hurt and harm that results when such statements and insinuations are made. Let us be fair and not make such rash statements that throw a shadow across the path of the divorced parent who is striving to overcome this kind of stigma for the sake of the children.

But if a nation is no stronger than its homes, we do right to ask what kind of chaos is America headed for in view of the fact that (at the time of this writing) it is believed that there are some three million or more American children of divorced parents.

Behavioral changes in the child of divorce will occur. Christian divorced parents can do much to forestall changes that would produce alienation from the church, or turn them against the Bible and God, or even make them turn on other Christians. Other lovingly concerned Christian friends and relatives can help in this regard, too. For instance, if a child of divorce sees a friend of his mother's reacting negatively to his mother, he may become embittered against that friend and blame Christianity. Great damage has been done. How unwise it is for Christian friends and relatives at such a time to take sides, to pit people against each other, and to speak their opinions when they cannot possibly know both sides of the story nor understand all that is involved. How much better it is for Christian friends to let it be known to the divorced couple and their children that they are genuinely sorry, but that they will continue to love them both and hold out understanding and love for the entire family. It is much easier to catch the look of love than it is to dodge the stones of castigation. Remember, some of those stones may hit our children; if not directly, they may bounce off us as we strive to defend ourselves.

One child of divorce states:

When Mom was unhappy or down, so were we. It hurt me to see her slighted by former friends—friends who had even advised her to get a divorce. When she did, where were they? But I felt guilty and angry. I had witnessed a lot of the fruit of the unhappiness this caused my Mom; I also knew what it had been like when she and Dad were together. Just remembering it even made me feel guilty.

This child of divorce was very articulate about her feelings:

My anger lasted a long time. I did terribly at school. But my schoolmates and teachers actually had nothing to do with my problems. I was just angry at everything that had happened, not angry at any one person, not even angry at my parents. I hated the breakup of my parents' marriage; but now I see it was better than living the way we were. Mom became a different person—relaxed, much more calm in her ways with us kids; she had more time for us and was much more loving. Dad became different, too. They both changed for the better—something they couldn't seem to achieve together. How can anyone say divorce is so wrong when it really did so much more for our parents, and I think in the long run for us kids?

But Mom's attitude made the difference. She helped us to see that you don't keep your eyes focused on people. People can let you down. Even she did at times, but she would apologize and admit that things were kind of tough and she got lonely, and she just asked us to bear with her and to understand. We made it out of that maze, but it was our faith in God that pulled us through. He never once let us down. Both Mom and Dad had to remind us pretty often to keep on keeping on with God.

No other persons, regardless of how skilled they may be, or how knowledgeable they may think they are, can predict what lifelong impact the breakup of a family has on children. It is believed that often the imprint in some cases is so indelible that it deeply alters permanently their behavior and their life patterns.

> What is suspected—and documented by observation—is that children learn by example. What they learn or fail to learn—because of the breakup of the family unit which gave them their stability—could impair their future ability to function as parents themselves. . . .
> A broken home can critically change the course of a child's learning experience by missed opportunities not easily recallable. That is why a stable family life is critically important and why there can be no social progress without it. . . .
> Easily the most bitter and damaging fruit of a broken home—and a pattern common to many children of divorce—is instability. It can dog a child through life.[5]

It cannot be denied that the harvest from many a broken home is children who develop into unstable adults who marry young—repeating their parents' mistake in their own efforts to regain lost security in their desperate search for love.

But to be aware of this pattern is to be forearmed, and the truly conscientious divorced parent will do all he or she possibly can to help his or her children through difficult years and try to counsel and guide them in making important lifetime choices. I believe that the divorced Christian parents I talked to are making determined efforts to ease their children through the turmoil caused by the divorce and are prayerfully seeking to reestablish stable, one-parent homes.

The Christian community can help by giving such parents a chance, by not prejudging them and setting up impossible barriers which must be overcome and obstacles that would impede their progress with their children.

According to a study by Dr. Judson T. Landis, professor of family sociology, divorce tends to run in families, and the children of divorce tend to go steady with, become engaged to, and marry others from divorced families because they have so much in common.

Another significant conclusion that his study revealed is that continued home conflict harms a child more than a divorce, and that it is not the divorce but rather the unhappy home situation that determines how a child faces life.

This is substantiated by others in the field of family relations.

Contrary to what many people think, divorce is not as difficult on some children as is often supposed. This is not to say that there is not unhappiness and a sense of loss and other emotional feelings involved; but it is to recognize that where unpeace has been evident so long in a home, the children are conditioned to pain and hurt. Marriage counselors, family guidance clinics, psychologists, and specialists are now agreeing that it is mounting discord within the home between marriage partners that brings on the problems retarding healthy development of children. It is not always the process of divorce as such.

Ralph P. Bridgman, chief marriage counselor at the Family Court Center, Toledo, Ohio, has written that divorce is often preferable to uncontrolled and unabated discord. Marital discord and estrangement always retards and often reverses the processes of personality fulfillment in partners and always imposes hazards upon the healthy development of children. Examination of figures leaves no doubt that the failure of partners to adjust to each other in marriage is related to unhappiness, twisted values, emotional disturbance, and delinquency in their children.

Dr. Richard A. Gardner, New Jersey psychiatrist, says statistics reveal that a bad marriage is usually harder on children than no marriage:

> The incidence of psychic disturbance in children of an unhappy but intact marriage is significantly higher than for children of broken marriages. If parents ask my advice whether they should divorce, I have to tell them that the statistics are on their side. But for any individual child, you cannot predict.[6]

For my children I cannot predict. For your children neither can you, nor can anyone else. Today many children of divorce are living in a more peaceful situation than when their parents were together. Is saving a marriage for the children sufficient reason to keep a relationship together? There are many who feel it is, and so they do. But the incidence of divorce among couples in their middle to late forties and upward is increasing, due, it is believed, to the fact that many couples are divorcing after the children have left the family nest—gone to college, gone into military service, gone out on their own working, or gotten married. What does this reveal? The fact that in many homes the marital situation has been less than ideal while the children were at home. What this has done through the years to come to some of their children time alone will tell. It does explain why many young people in the somber light of their parents' bitter experiences are wary of making any such commitment in marriage themselves; they call marriage a disaster and so we see them living together instead of marrying.

While we recoil in horror as Christians at this, many young people in all honesty believe it is the better way. We cannot condone this, and it is unscriptural; but what we must recognize is their desire to be honest. They hate the hypocrisy they have seen in their parents and other adults, and they are backing off from any such pretense. Somehow as loving, concerned adults we must get through to our own children that this is not the answer.

Dr. Gardner, the New Jersey psychiatrist who has written the book of advice for children of divorced parents, has some advice for their parents, too. The advice is basically the same: communicate. He urges parents to be "appropriately truthful" about their divorce and to share "thoughts and feelings of mutual concern" with their children. His advice is to make the divorce a complete severance if damage to the children is to be minimized. "Make divorce a fait accompli," he states. "The breaking of the neurotic tie with the ex-spouse is an important determinant in whether the divorce will be salutary for the children."[7]

The two most common neurotic ties that divorced people exhibit are the search for revenge and the attempt at reconciliation. In this kind of tug-of-war, it is the children who invariably get torn. Dr. Gardner does not believe parents should stay married for the sake of the children. In the book he advises children to "be very careful to believe only those things (that parents say about each other) that you are very sure of, or that you see yourself."[8]

The best answer a child can give to one or the other of the parents who questions them about whether the other is dating or spending a lot of money is to answer: "Please stop trying to turn me into a tattletale."[9]

We do our children a great injustice when we make them the victims of our own tragic marital mistake. We need rather to help our children, especially through the initial weeks, months, and even years, of making the right adjustment. Spending time with them is good for them and for ourselves. Making certain they spend time with others their age is essential, and entering into sports activities, school functions, church and other outings with them is time invested wisely.

A Washington, D.C., attorney, Newton Frohlich, who has handled hundreds of divorce cases, says, "Parents who stay together under loveless and discordant circumstances are likely to see their children grow in size but damaged in psyche." This attorney believes, as most everyone would, I am certain, that the best solution to marital problems is to repair the damage and reunite the family; however, the alternative solution in relationships that are "dead" is divorce.

"Every year more than half a million American couples decide to end their marriages," Frohlich says, adding, "And a serene broken home may be better for children than an unhappy unbroken home."[10]

Dr. John B. Reinhart, child psychologist, says that on the scale of childhood crises, divorce in the family is second only to the unexpected death of a parent. Does the child of divorce need to move the rest of his life along a trail of emotional wreckage? Certainly not! There is the initial shock, a period of disbelief and protest, but then a gradual healing takes place. This happens not only for the children, but for the couple involved. Yes, there will be scar tissue, and healing takes time. Reinhart believes that for the children of divorce, "Life is never quite the same." Christian parents, however, have it within their power to control what happens in their divorce situation.

Difficulties can be overcome, happiness is possible, life can still be meaningful and beautiful—these are things we can teach our children even though they are children of divorce. We don't achieve this in our own strength; we do it, as the Bible says, with the help of God. All things are possible, "all that happens to us can work for our ultimate good, if we love God and will fit into his plans" (Rom. 8:28). We may not have achieved this in our marriage, and we do not blame God; we have only ourselves to blame—this we can teach our children too. But it doesn't mean that the rest of our lives have to be spent in morbid looking back, in unhealthy, mournful retrospection.

The Bible tells us to press on, to move on to the mark "of the high calling of God in Christ Jesus" (Phil. 3:14, *AV*). We, with our children, can hold firmly to the truths we know and profess to believe. Just because we have failed in this aspect of our lives does not mean failure is to be the pattern for the rest of our lives. God is too just, too merciful, too loving to allow this to impede us for the rest of our days here upon earth. Others of his creatures fail him in other ways; his own disciples let him down, as did many of the Old Testament heroes and heroines of the faith. He doesn't love us any less than he did them; God is in the restoring and transforming business, and people are his first priority.

With regard to the practical aspects of divorce—the one who retains custody of the children should do all within his or her ability to see to it that the children are not deprived of spending time with the other parent. The parents must recognize that while they are, in a sense, retreating from the marriage relationship through divorce, they cannot ever retreat from the fact that they do have children. Someone has said, "Forget the marriage relationship as it once existed, but don't forget your children." Our children are living realities and proof of a relationship we may prefer to forget, but forget them we must not do.

The most painful aspect of divorce is the fact that the one who does not retain custody does not get to see his (or her) children every day. His or her role in the child's life will be different; but it can still be vital and important. Our children have the right to be the child of both parents; we must not deprive them of that right through our own selfish and self-centered desires. We must at all times strive to be reasonable. Communicate, consult, and cooperate are three essentials. Even though we may not have been able to do that within the confines of our marriage relationship, still, if we both seek the best for our children, then we must do so after the divorce. This can be achieved. My former husband and I have and are doing so. I consult him, for instance, regarding dental and doctor appointments. When one of the children is taking a trip, we apply the three essentials of communication, consultation, and cooperation. The telephone is as near as my arm's ability to extend, just as it is for him. And, when necessary, we consult each other in person. All of this has helped to ease the adjustment for the children.

When it is necessary, as it often is, for the wife to return to work, it is important that the former husband keep in mind the children's mother is putting forth extra effort. She needs opportunity to relax and to be free from the children at given times. One of the greatest things a father can do for his children is to give them a happy mother. If you could not achieve that in marriage, you now have the opportunity to do so. It can only make her a better mother to your children. The children must not be made to feel that their mother is running out on them, but it is a known fact that we all need a change of pace. The mother also needs the companionship of other adults, and when this involves going out with other men and the children and former husband know it, the children should not be pumped for information about their mother's activities. Keeping in mind the children's happiness and best mental health is all-important. Both parents need to remember this and put aside their own personal feelings, prejudices and curiosity.

I speak from experience when I say that a woman who has to keep her children under control while holding down a job and laboring under the stigma of divorce is going through a tremendous period of adjustment. She needs all the help and encouragement she can get from Christian friends, relatives, and even her former mate. Just so, the divorced father needs that supportive treatment that Christian charity at its best will always give forth. Neither should deny this right to the other.

There is nothing to be gained by antagonizing your ex-partner. Doing what you know is objectively right even though your emotions may try to tell you to do something else will in the end result in the least hurt and psychological damage to your children. Our focus should be on doing what is most constructive and rewarding for the child. In the final analysis, we ourselves stand to also gain from that kind of attitude. We make it easier to live with ourselves. Granted it is not easy to always be magnanimous about one's ex-husband or ex-wife. We must remember that children are children—we should not expect them to understand adult emotions, nor do we have any right to make them grow up sooner than their time by making them experience our pain. It is enough for them to cope with their own pain.

It has been estimated that the average American father spends a total of two hours a week with his child. The divorced father is often given many more hours weekly, depending upon the visitation rights granted to him. But even where the court dictates something less than weekly rights and the father wishes to see his children more often, maintaining a cordial relationship with his ex-wife can insure his spending more time with the child or children. How important it is to make wise use of such time together. How enriching and satisfying this can be for each of you. Don't, however, make the mistake of pampering the child, loading him with all sorts of goodies, spoiling him, and letting him "use" you. He needs your companionship, your emotional support, your interest in his school and other activities, your love and guidance. In you he needs more than a pal; he still needs a father, someone with whom he can share confidences.

What does divorce do to children? Even as I write this book my eleven-year-old son is showing a tender concern for me. "Mother, when will you be finished writing whatever it is you're writing?" His arms entwined themselves around my neck. "I don't want you working so hard. I don't want you going blind. When I go to Canada on my vacation I'm going to worry about you being here all by yourself. Will you promise me you won't work all the time?" Tears flowed (mine) as he walked out the door, his back to me. Momentarily I *was* blind!

Would he have developed such thoughtfulness and consideration if he had not experienced some suffering along the way? Yes, I would spare him pain and undue suffering; yet, even as it is true for myself that I have come through deep water and not been drowned, even so God has answered my prayers, and this child's sensitivity will go with him all through life. Someday I expect him to show that same thoughtfulness and consideration to a wife he can love and cherish.

It is difficult in a one-parent home to do all the things we'd like to do; it is difficult to exercise the right amount of discipline—I have a tendency to be too easy on my children. There is a danger in this; somehow we are prone to do this, feeling we must compensate. It is a serious mistake to give in to a child's every whim and allow too much freedom and independence. Children learn primarily by imitation and example. The way you handle your emotions will greatly determine your child's ability to cope. Among heavy drug-users in young people, it has been discovered that there is usually a history of poor parent-child relations, as well as poor interparent relations and a disorganized and unhappy family life. Drugs and alcohol are forms of escape. If you are resorting to such means to "solve" your own problems, you can be almost certain you are setting the stage for your child to follow in your steps.

If your child shows evidence of personality disorders, or if the schoolteacher and his report card give evidence that he may be having some problems, you would be wise to seek professional help. Children of divorce can develop new strengths as they make the adjustment to divorce; but it is not a sign of failure on your part to seek counsel from experts should the need arise. Do not let your own pride stand in the way of admitting that you and your child may need psychotherapy. Do not underestimate the role of psychological counseling and counselors. When it is necessary to obtain such help, do try to make certain you have the help of a Christian trained in these areas.

There is another area that needs to be discussed. It has to do with teaching our children about sex and love. Where there are happy male-female (husband-wife) family relationships, the children learn by observing their parents and by seeking answers about sex from both. Just because we have failed in this area does not mean our children need to develop negative attitudes. In spite of our divorce, we can teach our children that beautiful love relationships are possible to achieve. Our daughters need to know that somewhere out there in God's world there is a right man for them. Our sons need to know that there is a right woman awaiting them. Neither our sons nor our daughters should be conditioned to distrust the opposite sex; but we can teach them what desirable characteristics to look for that will make a man a good husband and father and will insure that a woman qualifies for being a good wife and mother. The Bible has much to say on the subject of sexual conduct and the role of husbands and wives. We must make certain that our children do not remain ignorant about the facts of life, and that they hear them correctly from us.

Among my clippings is an anguished letter written by a ten-year-old to a superior court judge. Her parents were seeking a divorce. The letter said, "Please, please help a ten-year-old keep a Mom and Dad. . . ." It was a plaintive plea that caused many, I am certain, to be shaken, just as the judge said he was. I could not agree more that divorce is difficult for children—their anguish is real. What we must realize is that sometimes in order for a mom and dad to be kept, the marriage must go. Through the anguish of the dissolution of the marriage, children such as this must be loved and loved and loved some more.

I would hope and pray that this chapter has helped to focus on the other side of divorce as it affects children and their parents. In so doing I have striven to give a balanced view to help the reader understand and to be better able to relate to those around him who are divorced.

> Married couples who decide to stay together "for the sake of the children" and then continue to mistreat one another verbally and physically make a grave mistake. No doubt, they decide to stay in the unhealthy marriage for themselves, not their children, because if they had their children's best interests at heart, they would either change their destructive treatment of one another and learn to live happily, or dissolve the marriage and try to live as happy individuals, each giving the children his best. There is overwhelming evidence that children who live in homes split by emotional divorce (undivorce) are generally worse off than children whose parents separate and obtain a legal divorce.[11]

I agree with that statement on the basis of my own experience. I am convinced that I am a better mother now than I ever was during the twenty-plus years of marriage. I am not saying the fault lay entirely with my husband; I am admitting, instead, to gross failure on my part. Today I find myself able to relate to my children in a much more meaningful way—I am more loving, much more honest with them, have much greater patience, and am much more concerned about their total welfare. In fact, there are so many "much mores" that apply that it would be difficult to enumerate them all.

This is not to say that I am advocating that raising children in a one-parent home is the ideal, or that it is even better. "There is no better way to rear children than in a home with two mature, sane, reasonable adults who love one another and their children."[12] That is a statement I would uphold and defend to my dying day. The best assurance against divorce, it has been stated by Billy Graham and others, is to have a Christ-centered home. That is an absolute truth.

Somehow some of us fail to achieve God's ideal. It does not mean we do not have Christ in our lives; we are imperfect human beings and willing to admit it. "If the choice is between having the children live with both parents when the parents are consistently miserable and neurotic together or with one parent who can behave in a more reasonable way, I believe that the children fare better with the one happy, rational parent."[13] There is truth in that statement.

And so some of us are divorced and we have children—they are often called "the children of divorce." We are working to rebuild our lives and theirs, and seeking God's guidance so that our children are not permanently warped and maimed by our failures and mistakes. Can readers understand this other side of divorce? And even if you cannot fully comprehend, can you leave the matter in God's hands and ours and not add to our problems?

Just as this chapter reached conclusion so did our eleven-year-old son's Little League baseball season. He was the pitcher for his team and received the most valuable player of the year team award; in addition, his team took the All-City Championship, winning over twenty-eight other teams. My former husband and I attended every game; we yelled and cheered our son on along with other parents. Everyone had a great time. I, as a mother, felt tremendously rewarded when

Kraig's father said to me, "You've done a fantastic job with that boy; he's a wonderful kid!"

I had prayed long and earnestly over this particular chapter in this book. The book has been a difficult undertaking, but this chapter weighed heavily on my heart. My former husband's comment at that ball game was as though God laid his hand of blessing on this chapter. It meant a great deal. Later, as I shared this with our married son, he said, "Mom, it's true; Kraig's come through the divorce okay."

THINK ON THESE THINGS

A twelve-year-old girl wrote the following letter to Ann Landers. It contains food for thought.

I am a twelve-year-old girl who has something to say to a lot of kids who are in the same spot I'm in. My parents are divorced.

I'm the youngest of four kids. We all live with Mom, but we see Dad every two weeks and write him letters whenever we feel like it. This might not be nice to say, but I'm glad my folks got a divorce. When Dad was home, he and Mom fought all the time and it made us kids very nervous. Mom had headaches and Dad had stomachaches. Now they both feel fine and treat each other like friends instead of enemies.

Us kids feel better, too. My little brother has stopped stuttering and I don't shake like I used to when I was afraid my dad might lose his temper and slap my mother.

So, kids, if your parents are separated or divorced, it probably means they had to do it for their health's sake and for yours, too. So cheer up and don't feel sad.

That letter was signed "I understand."

Children are people, too, and they can come through the crisis of divorce. Children are tremendously resilient, and if adults will exercise the kind of understanding this child demonstrated, then there can be happiness and a bright future for the children of divorce.

Our responsiblity is to encourage the right at all times, not to hope for evil (2 Cor. 13:8).

10
Remorse? Or Triumph?

"You will be interested to learn that———is in the process of suing his wife for divorce on the grounds of incompatibility. This seems to be becoming quite a popular pastime among Christians." The letter hit me like the blow of a sledge-hammer. How could anyone possibly feel that divorce was a popular pastime! The dictionary tells me that a pastime is a way of spending spare time; anything done for amusement, recreation, or diversion. Divorce a popular pastime? The thought made me gag; I felt nauseated, sick to the very pit of my stomach. Obviously the writer of the letter—a friend—had never experienced the trauma of divorce either personally or in the life of a close family member. My heart ached for him. The Bible says Moses allowed divorce because of the hardness of men's hearts; but at that moment, as I reread the letter, I had the awful feeling that divorced people weren't the only ones who had hard hearts.

I wrote a letter in reply. It was never sent. I could not bring myself to reply to that letter, I would leave the matter in God's hands. Now, however, as I write this book, in going through my materials I have come across that tear-streaked unfinished letter.

Dear———:
Contrary to what you said, divorce is not a popular pastime. While I respect your judgment on most matters, and have always had you on a pedestal in my

thinking, I cannot agree with your views on divorce. Yes, I know what the Bible says and I love God's Word.

I feel very sorry for both———and his wife. I know what they are going through and it is not pleasant or popular from the standpoint of something one likes to do.

I don't know the circumstances surrounding the ———'s decision, but I don't need to in order to hold out love to *both* of them. People who go through divorce do not need criticism nor judgmental attitudes heaped upon them by well-meaning Christians. I do not expect you to understand their situation any more than you can understand ours.

For years I prayed asking God to straighten out our marriage and to give me back the love for my husband that I once felt I had. I not only prayed for this, but worked at it. We both did. I am not blaming God for what has happened—there had to be a willingness on my part; but something was destroyed, gone—I accept the blame.

I also prayed about divorce, seeking God's will regarding *our* particular situation, and I put out a fleece. Within three days God answered in a way so definite I dared not retract. God has provided and he has blessed. Through it all I have experienced peace down deep, deep within—not always peace with some of God's people, but peace with God . . .

The letter remained unfinished, smudged with tears, and was laid aside.

I have shared with certain individuals my experience relative to "putting out a fleece" and have been criticized for this. I do value and respect the opinions of these Christian friends, many of whom have a background of Bible school and much theological training. I am not a theologian; I make no pretense of having the answers to theological issues. At the time I "put out a fleece," I had a simple faith and trust in God, just as I do now. If I had it to do all over again, I would still put out a fleece. I did not question then whether it was theologically sound and correct. All I knew was that I was desperate. If I did something wrong, it was not deliberate. I remembered Gideon in desperate straits—Gideon who was considered a mighty man of valor, yet who considered himself the least in his Father's house (Judg. 6:12, 15). I felt a kinship to this godly man; the story always held a special fascination for me—I would do what Gideon did.

I have since read and been told that now, under the dispensation of the Spirit, we are not to expect signs before our eyes (as Gideon asked for and received in Judg. 6:36–40). But instead we must earnestly pray to God that if we have found grace in his sight, he would show us a sign in our heart, by the powerful operations of his Spirit there, fulfilling the work of faith, and perfecting what is lacking in it. In my own heart, once the decision was made, I did experience peace. (I still find myself, however, even now putting out "fleeces.") It seemed confirmation that I was doing what had to be done under the circumstances, and it was not unusual to meet someone on the street, in the market or while shopping, in the months following, and have them say to me, "You look so different—what have you done?" Others would say, "You look peaceful."

There were those, however, who could not comprehend the look of peace nor the fact that I wasn't running around wringing my hands, crying on everyone's shoulder, or showing remorse in other demonstrative ways. I had made up my mind at the outset that I would not inflict our marital woes upon others, nor the problems relating to the actual divorce. I did not wish to say things about my former mate. I respected his business judgment. We had our differences, but they were ours; no need to pitchfork them onto others. I walked out of my friends' lives with deliberate intent. I did not want them to have to choose sides. My thinking was that they knew where I lived, my telephone number had not changed, and if they wished to see me they knew how they could reach me. Busyness is good therapy; I heartily recommend it to divorced women. I already knew from years of keeping busy that this was healthy. I would keep busy. You would not find me gulping pills in order to get through the day or to cope with matters at hand. I did not want to cop out; I prayed for the ability to cope. (Use medication if you must, but only under close supervision of your doctor and/or counselor.)

It was my good friend, Keith Miller—a highly successful writer noted for his honesty—who showed me my mistake in failing to contact and keep in touch with former friends. I am indebted to him for daring to be so honest with me. In a moment of sharing, I mentioned the fact that some of my former Christian friends had "walked out of my life." His reply was, "Who walked out of whose life?"

I stammered an answer, explaining what is written in a previous paragraph. We discussed this, and he was glad that so many friends did telephone, did make it a point to keep in close touch, and not only with me but with my former mate. With these friends there is now a friendship in depth which can only come as people walk together through deep water and the burning fire (that does not consume) experiences.

But there are those who do walk out of our lives when we walk out of theirs, and who may never walk back in. This is one of the things the divorced person must recognize. If our dependency is on other people and their opinions, then divorce will only complicate our lives and give us great distress. On the other hand, there are those who will stand by with words of understanding, encouragement, and love. They are the salt of the earth; this is not to say that the others are not "salty" in their own way in other aspects of their Christian life, but their saltiness will not touch our lives. That is their choice—this is what I recognized—and I still feel it is better not to inflict our problems upon others, forcing them to become involved. I should have kept in better touch with some of my former friends, however, explaining my actions, and stating that I didn't want them involved but still valued their friendship. As far as I am concerned, they are still friends, and I do not fault them for their seeming lack of communication with me. The lack has been on my part.

Remorse? Is that quality lacking in the lives of those who seek divorce? I recall with inner pain the incident that occurred some months after the divorce was final. The children and I were having dinner in a local restaurant. It was a lovely place; the lights were dim, and we had decided this would be a special night out for the three of us. We were escorted to our booth, and we sat chatting. I was mostly listening as I unwound from the day's work. My attention was diverted to a familiar-sounding voice in the next booth. The children continued talking to each other, but my ears were tuned to the conversation in the other direction. "I can't understand it, when you see her and talk to her she doesn't even show remorse." Someone else questioned, "How long has the divorce been final?" I switched my tuning to the children's conversation. It was much more edifying.

Eavesdropping, I decided then and there, was strictly for the birds! A sense of humor is tremendously important if one is to maintain his balance. I dared to ask God to help me keep mine. I'm inclined to think God has a sense of humor, too, and there were many times he had me smiling—sometimes through tears, but they were not tears of bitterness.

Let me just say by way of explanation that the previous week the children and I had been to that same restaurant for dinner and had met this gentleman by surprise. He invited us to share his booth, which we did. In the course of eating our dinner he'd asked how things were going and I'd replied, "Just fine." We discussed briefly the divorce and what had happened. I asked him how he was and inquired about his wife. Later I learned that she was in a mental institution.

God is such a good teacher. He has taught me so many

valuable lessons in these past difficult years. I learned an invaluable lesson that night in that restaurant; how unwise we are to think we can read what's going on in another person's heart and mind! Was there no remorse in my heart? Is divorce a popular pastime?

They say that the best justification for divorce is that all individuals involved come out winners, not losers. I am reminded of the minister who so graciously shared this experience with me. He said:

> My wife told me that the day would come when I would thank her for seeking the divorce. I didn't accept it at the time. I didn't believe that day would ever come, but the time has come now, after approximately two years. She was absolutely right, and I'm grateful to be out of the marriage, which was not satisfying to either one of us. I wish her the very best, and I know she wishes the very best for me. We are good friends, although we do not see each other. If she were in need, I would want to—not just feel an obligation—but I would want to be of help to her. I'm certain she feels the same towards me. Both of our lives are now more satisfying apart rather than together.

Are divorced people supposed to spend the rest of their lives in remorse? I do not believe God would have us wasting our time in sick retrospection. Yes, of course, there is some remorse; no one gloats over past failure and sin. But let us get on with life and with living. There is work to be done. Satisfying and rewarding work. Challenging work. No divorced person has to live feeling he is on the shelf for the rest of his or her life. God has a place and a plan for his children. We who are divorced are not excluded.

What was Jesus saying with regard to divorce? Was he really rapping the Pharisees and Sadducees, those who wanted to put their wives away because they now were attracted to someone else? Was he definitive in all that he said about divorce? Or was there much left unsaid? If you take what Jesus said about love and the fact that he came that we might have abundant life, I ask you: How can an individual have the abundant life living in the misery of a marriage that is a disaster? The minister mentioned earlier said:

At the end of thirty years of marriage, we were in misery. I find it difficult to believe that a God of love wishes his children to remain in a marriage which is not a marriage. Some marriages are nothing but tyranny. Slavery of the worst kind for both individuals. God cannot be a loving Father and say, "Stay in this trial by fire forever." In fact, he could not be a God of love any more than you could be a devoted parent or I could, and continue to keep your son or daughter in a vitiating, negative, debilitating situation which was destroying them.

This is a form of biblical literalism that I cannot in all scholarship accept, because I do believe that there are areas of Scripture which are indicators, but they do not tell us what the context is. If divorce violates the loving tenderness of Jesus Christ that was so complete that there was a totality of sacrifice for mankind, how do you justify that in a rigid, Old Testament legalism? Jesus said that he hadn't come to change the law but to fulfill it. He came to add this dimension of love to the law.

If I want happiness for my children, does God? I have a freedom, I have a joy now that I didn't have in thirty years of married life. I believe this is what God wants for me. If he did not want this for me, would he not say so, would he not bring upon me that which deserves punishment? I have gotten none of that from God. I have had one blessing after another. There has been remorse; but there was more remorse in the marriage as it was. We could not make a triumph of our marriage, but we can make a triumph of the rest of our lives.

THINK ON THESE THINGS

A basic premise of Christianity is the fact that from tragedy can spring triumph. Should the divorced individual be faulted for demonstrating that kind of triumph?

The important thing for us as Christians is not what we eat or drink [Paul used these as examples] but stirring up goodness and peace and joy from the Holy Spirit. If you let Christ be Lord in these affairs, God will be glad; and so will others. In this way aim for harmony in the church, and try to build each other up (Rom. 14:17–19).

11
The New Dimension

Suppose you were a minister—you'd been dedicated to the Lord as an infant by your well-known minister father and your mother, you'd had an unusual chain of circumstances that led you to follow in the footsteps of your godly Father, you graduated from one of the country's finest theological seminaries and then went right into the ministry. You've always felt that there was an unseen but guiding hand over you. You were married. Your wife had always said while you were courting her that there would be two people she'd never marry, the one was a physician and the other was a minister because she didn't believe she'd have much time with either one of them and she wanted a lot of time with her husband. You agonized over that initial decision as to whether or not to go into the ministry. Your engagement with the girl of your choice was even broken off because of it. You did become reengaged, however, when she decided she could be a minister's wife after all.

Following the marriage you served in several churches—churches with much prestige and status. You had a good life and two children came along. But you were busy and often you felt your lives were going in different directions. You tried. She tried. Still this dichotomy of interests existed. You knew that the marriage was shredding more and more. And then it happened. The children were now well grown. After thirty years of married life your marriage came to an end.

Divorce!

The circumstances vary, but it's happening not only to the man and woman in the pew, but to clergymen as well. The *Los Angeles Times*[1] carried an article entitled "Higher Divorce Rate Hits Older Marriages," with the subtitle "More Durable Pairings Succumbing to Time; Lack of Communication Blamed." The article states that "till death do us part" became a traditional marriage vow years ago when a couple's life expectancy was only about twenty-five years beyond their wedding ceremony. But a Burbank, California, marriage counselor thinks that longer lives of married couples are contributing to a rising divorce rate.

"There is a national upsurge of divorces among couples who have been married twenty years or more," according to Dr. Harry Adams, working minister for the United Methodist Church, in speaking before a Van Nuys, California, meeting of the family law section of the Valley Bar Association.

What happens to a Christian minister when his marriage disintegrates and ends in divorce? Not all are as fortunate as the Orange County, California, divorced clergymen who shared their stories with me. One of these men stated:

> We need all kinds of help and healing, for we are living in a society of fractured relationships. No day goes by that I'm not now encountering someone who has either been through this or is going through it with someone else, standing by, trying to help. I pray that the Lord makes your book a volume that offers help and hope, and that it can be a blessing to the Christian church. The primary message that all of us as Christians must remember and must share with others is that there is one relationship that can never be fractured.
>
> The most remarkable thing about my own divorce experience has been the fact that my own relationship with God through Christ has gotten stronger and more

beautiful. No matter what I face in the future, no matter what any of your readers faces—and we can all face some very dark valleys in the shadow—God is right there with all his strength, greatness, and love. And it seems, especially these days, that most all of my prayers, except as I'm interceding for someone, are prayers of thanksgiving. I really can't ask God for much. He's already given me so much that I can't ask him for anything more.

I found that an amazing statement! Here was a minister of the Gospel sitting behind his desk in his church study, calm and composed, a very peaceful look on his face. Love radiated from his eyes, his hands were crossed, and his whole bearing was relaxed and confident. Yet, he was divorced. According to the critics of divorced Christians, shouldn't such as this gentleman be pacing back and forth, nervously twitching, evidencing great remorse and extreme anxiety? Here was a man whom the Christian world would say has lost his wife and—well, what about the "and his church"? Did he lose his position as a Christian minister?

He related what had happened.

It was a traumatic experience. I thought, "Well now, with losing my wife, will I also be losing my position as a Christian pastor?" So many churches just cannot take a divorced clergyman. I don't mind telling you I was nervous as a cat about that, because I wondered would I also be out of my calling in life? But this I would say has been the most remarkable thing that's happened to me in my life, and that has been the love, tenderness and affection my congregation has given me. I think the divorce took me off a pedestal! We all have "feet of clay." I knew it all along and never pretended that I was perfect. Now they knew it and I have received more genuine love and affection from my congregation than I've ever had really in the totality of my ministry prior to this.

I believe this minister has paid a well-deserved tribute to the people to whom he ministers. When I told him that, he said they deserved it.

I've preached many, many times about the love of God's people, but you always wonder if the chips were down yourself would you really receive it. And I have received it! There's no question about it, the church has accepted me as a divorced pastor.

As I remarked about his serenity he said:

There is a very positive side to divorce which Christians fail to acknowledge. All kinds of people in the congregation tell me I am a changed man, and that I've changed for the better—that I have become much more receptive to people's needs, that I am more openly tender. I believe what they are saying is true. Divorce very often changes people, and the changes I've seen are for the better.

This very wise and understanding pastor related some of his counseling experiences since his divorce. He told of a woman who shared an experience she'd had where her doctor had cried with her as she'd unburdened a terribly painful experience that happened in her life. The woman commented, "I was just almost healed by my doctor's tears." The divorced pastor talking to me said:

Helen, I cannot tell you how that struck me! All the people I'd counseled all these years in the ministry, and never once had I shed a tear with them! I don't know who wrote it, but somewhere one of the mystics used the phrase "the priceless gift of tears." I remembered that because I'd disagreed with it so sharply. Tears a gift? No way! That's sorrow! That's pain! That's hurt! That's bleeding! But that expression came to mind when this woman said to me, "I was just almost healed by my doctor's tears."

I began to do what I don't do often enough, but I'm now doing it with modest regularity—I took this before the Lord and asked him about it in my private devotions. Of course, you know the Lord sometimes doesn't say a word to you in an area, and he didn't say a word to me. But I noticed that later on my prayer changed. I began to ask him for *the gift of tears*. I still didn't hear any word from God on it; but in fact, it's now been several months ago when I first found myself crying with one of my parishioners—she was dying of cancer and as I opened up to her the great assurance of our faith and the Rock on which we stand, it was so meaningful to her, she began to cry. And so did I. My tears meant much to her it was obvious. That new dimension has come into my life which never would have come if it hadn't been this loving response I've received from this congregation as a result of my divorce.

Contrast that to an article written in a Christian magazine where the pastor was advised that if divorce happened to him it would be far better for the cause of Christ for him to give up the ministry permanently. This same article said, "Let the pastoral couple determine that they will let nothing come into their lives that will break up their marriage, and that they will endure all the disappointment, heartache, and suffering required to remain together until death forces their separation."[2]

The writer of this article states that the divorce problem is one of the thorniest, most delicate, and most frequent that the pastor has to face. A keen analysis. In our permissive society, the divorce rate continues to climb, he states.[3] His analysis is correct—divorce is thorny, delicate, and becoming more frequent. But it is unrealistic to tell pastoral couples to "endure" when the strong possibility exists that in so doing they become so hardened to each other that they fail to be sensitive to the needs of the people to whom they are called to minister. It would be difficult for such a pastor to minister and relate to a parishioner who is divorced or going through a divorce. My heart goes out to victims of divorce caught in a church situation like that.

The divorced minister quoted above says a new dimension has come into his experience as a result of the divorce and God's mercy shown through his people and in answer to prayer. He further related that shave time is his special prayer time.

> Every morning I'd pray the same prayer: "In Thee, O Lord, do I put my trust. Let me never be put to shame," quoting from the Psalms. No morning went by for months after the divorce action began and then after the divorce was final that I didn't pray the same thing. One morning I said, "Lord, you must be getting awfully tired of this prayer, but it's just on my heart and I've got to give it to you daily." I did and never was put to shame. In fact, I would say that during that period my faith was so magnificent. What came to me out of that faith I can never really adequately put into words, but the one sustaining sure thing in my life during that very difficult initial period of adjustment was God.

Actually this pastor's relationship to the Lord had always been a deep one. He'd spent a great deal of time studying the mystics, who were so helpful to him. But in his words:

It was just as though a curtain was lifted. It was as though I had a whole new picture of God and his nearness. Never during that period—and there would be terrible days, wearisome days—but never did my faith in God even have a tremor in it. My faith grew from strength to strength. God just always stood by me and so did his people.

The divorce has opened up vast new areas of concern and outreach to this southern California pastor and others like him to whom I talked. He states:

It is a paradox that I cannot fully understand. As an individual who could not make a triumph of his marriage, I am now literally inundated with people needing help in the area of their marital relationships. People feel that here is someone who knows what they are going through, and they think because I am a minister of the Gospel, as God's representative, I will not lie to them. And I don't. Actually my counseling ministry is tremendously expanded. It's a total surprise to me. I would think they would say, "Why talk to———? He couldn't make a go of his marriage."

This pastor's advice to couples seeking marital counseling who are on the verge of breaking up is the same as stated at the outset of this book. If you have any shred of love left for that man or woman, by all means build on it. Seek the help you need—professional counseling and spiritual help. Whatever it takes, if there's love left, work to build and repair it. God can take even that little shred, magnify it, and give it back to a couple in full bloom.

Does divorce for the Christian have to mean double death—death of the marriage and death of one's professional calling? The Christian minister quoted in this chapter faced that possibility; but there are others within the Christian circle who are not ministers who are also faced with the fact that no longer will they be allowed to serve on church boards, and so on. Their churches hold to a strict interpretation of 1 Timothy 3, which speaks of the qualifications of pastors (bishops) and deacons. There we read that a pastor must have only one wife, and the deacons must be the same sort of good, steady men as the pastors, with only one wife (verse 2).

One California pastor shared with me his experience when he came to the church he is serving. The church had gone through a purging and purifying in an effort to unite the body of Christ. Then it came time to decide what to do about the government of the church; up until this time it had been run by a board and a staff with no elders or deacons. This minister said:

> As I surveyed the scene I could not find one married couple under fifty that had not been involved in a multiple marriage. What was I to do? I knew what 1 Timothy 3 said. I consulted with the man whom I consider to be my own pastor. I also consulted three Greek scholars. It was the consensus that the original Greek said the pastor and deacons were to be husbands of one wife at a time. They were not to be polygamists. Today we have a wonderfully united body of believers who are one in Christ. I am the husband of one wife; I have never been divorced; but my deacons and elders are also husbands of one wife, though they have been involved in divorce.

I have visited in that church. I saw the love and oneness, a real "church as a body" concept.

THINK ON THESE THINGS

Personal growth for any of us—divorced or not—involves more than a few unhappy experiences and unsettling setbacks. Such experiences are often the prelude to a life of greater happiness and productivity. My idea of happiness may not necessarily coincide with yours (or vice versa), but it doesn't mean that my choices are wrong (or that yours are). We need to free ourselves from unwarranted guilt—by so doing new energies will be released into our lives to help us cope with the present (both its problems and its possibilities).

The Lord is good, a strong hold in the day of trouble; and he knoweth them that trust in him (Nah. 1:7, *AV*).

May God who gives patience, steadiness, and encouragement help you to live in complete harmony with each other—each with the attitude of Christ toward the other. And then all of us can praise the Lord together with one voice, giving glory to God, the Father of our Lord Jesus Christ (Rom. 15:5, 6).

12
Remarriage a No-No?

A divorced Christian college professor was told by numerous Christian colleges and Bible schools to which he applied for a position that he could teach in their schools so long as he did not remarry. Remarriage was out, for the most part, in many of these institutions. A few would make exceptions provided he remarried someone who had never been married before, or if he married a woman who had been previously married and divorced on "scriptural grounds." All this was, of course, provided he could prove his own divorce was granted on "scriptural grounds."

At the risk of being accused of sounding bitter, I would like to say that these same Christian colleges gladly accept financial support from their constituents and alumni— anyone interested in supporting their work even though they may be divorced and remarried. I and others to whom I have talked are on the mailing lists for several such colleges. We receive letters from them telling of their work and expansion programs and soliciting contributions. My money, and the money from others who are divorced—some remarried—is welcome; but we ourselves (some of us) are not. Such inconsistency of values cannot help but raise some questions. Is one's money of more worth than one's soul? How many divorced individuals have been sent away from Christian colleges and the church because of unyielding traditional views that have not been reexamined in the full light of Scripture that reveals not only God's judgment against sin, but Christ's love and acceptance of the sinner?

I think of one lovely young Christian coed who decided to marry a fine Christian man who was studying to be a minister. His wife had divorced him. When the coed made the decision to marry the young man, she was told she'd have to leave the school. This happened in her final year at the Bible college, within months of graduation. She was not allowed to finish school and graduate with her class.

There are many outstanding men and women in the Lord's work today who are having to shield the fact that they are divorced and remarried. If the general Christian public knew it, one wonders what it would do to their reputation. Would their books be bought? Would they be invited to speak and/or sing on campus, in the church, at conventions and religious gatherings? Many of these individuals defend themselves to those who do know on the ground that they were either divorced by their former mates after they became Christians, or they were divorced even before they became Christians. The Christian world has forced many divorced and remarried Christians to skirt the truth to avoid letting the facts be known.

But I would ask why should the man or woman who stayed in his or her bad marriage for many years, trying to hold it together because they were Christians and hated divorce—why should such as these be penalized for this when others didn't stick it out? Why not give them credit for trying? It is generally known, even by those who are not Christians, that divorce is frowned upon. The attitude of the Christian world has made many divorced Christians resort to the excuse that "they weren't really born-again Christians" when they sought the divorce. It shouldn't be necessary for the divorced person to have to stand in defense of himself every time he turns around, and have to provide reasons and/or excuses. He or she should be accepted on the basis that Christ accepts them. When the scarlet woman of the New Testament gave her heart to Jesus, he didn't demand to see her identification papers, nor have her undergo psychological tests; neither did he phone around checking her out. She was understood and accepted, and her only credential was that she provide herself, the sinner. Then he provided himself, the Savior.

I am not suggesting that the church, colleges, institutions, businesses founded on solid Christian principles, be lax in their set of standards; but why single out the divorced person, in particular that one who remarries or wishes to remarry, and impose upon him such a rigid set of rules? The same church, college, or Christians who say no to divorced remarried Christians, accept, read, quote and use the Book of Psalms. Yet David, who wrote many of the Psalms, was not only an adulterer, he was a murderer. He had another man killed so he could marry his wife. None of the divorced and remarried people whom I interviewed were guilty of that!

"The heart of a man is what really counts in the sight of God—not his history." This, of course, explains why God could say of David that he was a man after his own heart (Acts 13:12). When the prophet Samuel was sent by God to the home of Jesse to select a new king, the Lord said to Samuel, "Don't judge by a man's face or height, for this is not the way. I don't make decisions the way you do! Men judge by outward appearance, but I look at a man's thoughts and intentions"[1] (Sam. 16:7). God has divine vision; there isn't one of us who can make that claim.

C. S. Lovett, writing on this, says:

> This counsel to Samuel represents more than just a verse from the Old Testament; it is a deep and profound principle of Christian living. Any life that would please God must consider this principle, for there is no way to live pleasingly before God, if it is disregarded. The statement implies that all obedience unto God is from the heart.[1]

There are those who say that God said that about David while David was still a shepherd boy, before he fell into such great sin; but God sees the end from the beginning; he is a discerner of all our ways. The future is hidden from our limited gaze, but not from his. David's actions are not license for Christians to indulge in adultery, or to behave in other sinful ways. God's standards of right living haven't changed; neither has his vision. David paid for his sin in a costly, heartbreaking way.

Lovett goes on to say:

> What a thrilling revelation it is when the church can extend its arms to all men and say, "Come as you are and we will receive you in the name of Christ." This is the picture of Jesus that the church should present, for the non-judgmental Christ cannot be truly pictured by a discriminating church. The whole tenor of the church program becomes sweeter, and the way to fellowship and service is not barred at any point when the principle approach brings the church a new heart. What a horrible inconsistency when we say, "Come," and then throw up a barricade in the path of those with unfortunate marriage records. How many families have suffered hurt because of this ungracious procedure—to say nothing of the vast talent pool that has become idle and rusted. Many lives, bursting with gifts from God, could be salvaged through this change of heart.
>
> The story becomes even more exciting when the divorced person shares equal status with the gossipers, the hot-tempered deacons and elders, and the critical church gatherers. Then all can enjoy the same brand—just plain sinners. The pastor who can marry the ex-murderer and the wire-tapper, admitting them to church office, can, with equal conscience, marry and even

remarry, divorced individuals. They then become no different than the repentant swindler who gains a high place in the church. All are found to be of the same litter and in need of Jesus' sweet presence and the transforming power of His Word; they all stand in need of fellowship and service if they are to grow. In this kind of a church, Christ is offered as the Healer of broken hearts and His ministry reaches to every level. . . . What a reputation for the church to have—it consorts with sinners, publicans and harlots. Should any church fear to have the very same reputation as its Master—gentle and tolerant, hating the sin, but loving the sinner?[2]

But what about remarriage for divorced Christians? Those who take a firm stand disapproving of this point to the Scripture references already cited elsewhere in this book. The idea is often expressed that the divorced person who remarries is living in constant adultery. Is this really true? One outstanding Christian couple, well known and respected in the Christian world, receives letters from well-meaning Christians who know the man is divorced and remarried to a woman who was a widow. The letters tell them, "You are living in adultery."

If we carefully examine the words of Jesus in Matt. 19:9, we hear him say, "Anyone who divorces his wife, except for fornication, and marries another, commits adultery." Let us believe exactly what Jesus said, but let's not add anything to what he said. The dictionary definition of fornication as pertaining to the Bible means any unlawful sexual intercourse, including adultery. Jesus did not say that whosoever married after being divorced keeps on committing adultery. Nor did Jesus say that whoever marries her that was put away keeps on committing adultery. Adultery is an act, it is not a state one lives in. The Bible does not speak of "living in adultery." It speaks of "committing adultery."

The view has been expressed that when a divorced man or

woman remarries, the first time they are joined physically is an act of adultery, but after that they become one flesh in the sight of God. If it is his permissive will and they have been Spirit-led, from then on they are husband and wife. But for that first act there is forgiveness on the grounds that the blood of Christ at Calvary covers that sin, as well as other sins, and it is to be remembered against them no more.

In the Bible it would seem that a right to divorce carries with it the right to remarry. Of course this is understood and no objections are raised when it is known that a divorce was obtained on what is called "scriptural grounds." In Deut. 24:1, 2, we see very plainly that the legal annulment of a marriage meant the legal right to marry again. In this instance divorce was allowed on grounds other than adultery; because, for that, a woman was to die. But this reason was "some uncleanness in her."

It is known that the men of Moses' day, and those who subscribed to that law after Moses' time, abused this law regarding divorce, just as marriage vows are trampled upon today and divorce is not too difficult to obtain. But we are not here concerning ourselves with the abuse of divorce as practiced today by those who are not confessing Christians. We are speaking, rather, of those Christians who have gotten divorced only after great and serious consideration of the consequences; those Christians who have made a definite and dedicated effort to hold their marriages together; those Christians who for one reason or another did obtain a divorce, even though not on "scriptural grounds"; who arrived at the point where it was felt this was the better way. Should such as these be denied the right to remarry? Should individuals who have lived in spiritual adultery but who now seek release from that which has been so damaging to their soul—should they be looked upon with disdain and suffer discrimination at the hands of the church and the Christian world?

What did Jesus say? In Matthew 5, Christ begins his

121

Sermon on the Mount. In the context of that great message to the multitudes, the overall thrust of the words of Christ has to do with the higher law of love. In illustration after illustration he shows them that the law is subordinate to love. His emphasis is on the necessity of doing good for evil. He touches upon one specific area of a marriage relationship, alluding to the Old Testament law found in Deuteronomy 24, which speaks of "putting away one's wife." We must remember that the Pharisees were desirous of tripping Jesus up in terms of the law. They were talking about adultery. It is on the prohibition of retaliation for evil that Christ in this section is taking such a positive stand.

If women today think they have it bad, they should have lived in the Old Testament days, and in Jesus' time. One wonders how far women's liberationists would have gotten in that particular era of time. Jesus was aware that women in that culture were considered second-class citizens. They had very few rights. Therefore, Jesus is actually excoriating the Jews, denouncing strongly the fact that men were putting away their wives for even burning water, for the slightest trumped-up situation. He comes on full force and says:

> The law of Moses says "If anyone wants to be rid of his wife, he can divorce her merely by giving her a letter of dismissal." But I say that a man who divorces his wife, except for fornication, causes her to commit adultery if she marries again. And he who marries her commits adultery (Matt. 5:31, 32).

Jesus saw the inferior position of women, and he attempted to raise the level of his listeners' thinking. In God's sight, women are entitled to the same rights as men; but in the Jewish system, the wife had few rights. In the ancient world things were infinitely worse—according to Roman and Greek law the wife had absolutely no rights. The philosopher Cato once said that if you were to catch your wife in adultery, you could kill her with impunity without any court judgment. But if the man were involved in adultery, the woman would not dare to lift a finger against him, because the law forbade it. It is against this background that Jesus refers to divorce.

In the Christian Protestant world, evangelicals and fundamentalists, Bible-believing Christians, make a strong point about the necessity of reading Scripture in context, not quoting out of context, and so on. We cling very tenaciously to that thesis. Yet, when it comes to the matter of divorce, very rarely does one hear or read an explanation that makes clear the background around which particular statements in the Bible referring to divorce are made.

If we apply that principle here in terms of the Matthew and Mark passages on divorce, then we see Jesus speaking out against the legalism of the Pharisees who were testing him. He was giving the definition of the ideal marriage, which, it would be generally agreed among Christians, should be permanent and the union of two into one. Jesus was striking out at their quibbling and hairsplitting over what Moses said to do. They were using Moses as a legalistic dodge, and it was this legalism that Jesus exposed. There are very few passages in the Gospels where Jesus strikes out more against legalism than this one. If we go beyond the boundaries of what this verse is talking about, are we not caught up in the same kind of spirit that the self-righteous Pharisees had?

Jesus did not go into a lengthy explanation about all the different things that enter into a marriage relationship. There is much more to marriage than sex; there is much more that contributes to a bad marital relationship than the possibility of one or another of the marriage partners feeling the necessity for dissolving the marriage because his or her partner was having an adulterous affair. The passages referred to in the Bible which speak of divorce do not begin to cover all the many serious problems which enter into a marriage relationship that may lead to divorce. There are many who believe Jesus' teachings here are to be interpreted within the proper framework of an isolated kind of problem where men had total freedom to put away their wives, according to Jewish law. There is a much higher law to which the Christian subscribes.

What is that higher law? Is it not the fact that Jesus, as the personification of God's love, came to fulfill that law—the law which God himself authored? And we who name the name of Christ, who call ourselves Christians because we are his followers, seek to live according to his example. As it relates to divorce and remarriage, Jesus did not come and amend the original statute regarding marriage and divorce. If he had done that, then God would be correcting himself. God is perfect, and his laws, which are a reflection of his perfection, are perfect, too. How then could Jesus fulfill the law about marriage? He could do nothing other than to uphold the perfect standard.

Jesus pointed out that the trouble wasn't with the law, but in the fact that sinful man just cannot keep the law. God saw that he had a perfect law resting upon imperfect men. The Apostle Paul explains this in his letter to the Galatians: "Knowing that a man is not justified by the works of the law, but by the faith of Jesus Christ" (chap. 2:16a). Speaking to his Jewish brothers, Paul explains:

> We Jewish Christians know very well that we cannot become right with God by obeying our Jewish laws, but only by faith in Jesus Christ to take away our sins. And so we, too, have trusted Jesus Christ, that we might be accepted by God because of faith—and not because we have obeyed the Jewish laws. For no one will ever be saved by obeying them. . . . We are sinners if we start rebuilding the old system . . . of trying to be saved by keeping Jewish laws, for it was through reading the Scripture that I came to realize that I could never find

God's favor by trying—and failing—to obey the laws. I came to realize that acceptance with God comes by believing in Christ. I have been crucified with Christ and I myself no longer live, but Christ lives in me. And the real life I now have within this body is a result of my trusting in the Son of God, Who loved me and gave Himself for me. I am not one of those who treats Christ's death as meaningless. For if we could be saved by keeping Jewish laws, then there was no need for Christ to die (vs. 16, 18b–21).

Time after time Jesus had to do things that arbitrated against the law. Remember the occasion on the Sabbath day when Jesus and his disciples walked through corn fields and the disciples picked some of the corn. The Pharisees challenged Jesus on that. What was Jesus' answer? He said:

> Didn't you ever hear about the time King David and his companions were hungry, and he went into the house of God and they ate the special bread only priests were allowed to eat? That was against the law too. But the Sabbath was made to benefit man, and not man to benefit the Sabbath. And I, the Messiah, have authority even to decide what men can do on Sabbath Days! (Mark 2:25–28).

If David, incidentally, had actually been convicted of doing what he did, the Jewish law said the death penalty should be inflicted. In this instance, back in Old Testament times, the preservation of David's life was far more important than preserving the bread! Jesus taught this principle— that people are more important than rules and rituals—in his life here upon earth, and he demonstrated it through his actions.

Elsewhere in this book I have shown Jesus' attitude to the woman taken in adultery and to her accusers. Jesus deliberately set aside the letter of the law in this instance—by which law he himself could have picked up the first stone to hurl at her, especially since he was without sin. But he was more concerned that he fulfill the law and save her. Here we see that the higher law of love saved an individual. "Blessed are the merciful," said Jesus in his Sermon on the Mount (Matt. 5:7, *AV*). And his commandment to us is, "Be ye therefore merciful, as your Father also is merciful" (Luke 6: 36, *AV*).

On what authority does the Christian world today denounce the remarried Christian who is honestly seeking to live for the Lord? Surely not by the example of Jesus Christ in his dealings with people and as he viewed and applied the law. In my interviewing sessions with divorced and remarried Christians, I could not find one individual whose life was less productive as a result of divorce and remarriage. On the contrary, everyone with whom I talked felt their Christian walk was much closer to the Lord now than when they lived in spiritual adultery, in a state of undivorce.

Another minister related to me that the whole Book of Romans opened up to him in an entirely new way after his divorce and as he sought the Lord's will later regarding marriage.

My preaching took on new significance. Finally I was able to minister to people. There was a new openness to my preaching, an honesty I never had before. I couldn't hide my marriage failure, and ministers aren't supposed to have problems; yet, here I was—divorced. The day came when I stood before them in the pulpit and I could honestly say, "I only stand before you a Christian by the grace of God and as a minister by the grace of God." I quoted at length to them from Romans—Paul, you see, was talking about me!

Is there unrighteousness with God? Does God wink at divorce and remarriage? Does he not mean what he says about the two? Did Jesus make a mockery of his Father's words and the law? Paul writes:

> For he [God] saith to Moses, I will have mercy on whom I will have mercy, and I will have compassion on whom I will have compassion. So then it is not of him that willeth, nor of him that runneth, but of God that sheweth mercy (Rom. 9:15, 16, *AV*).

This same minister revealed to me that when he first went into the ministry, he would not remarry a divorced person. He related the struggle that went on in his soul—how his whole upbringing was such that you just didn't divorce. But then the mercy and grace of God broke over him; the love of Jesus came through, and he saw this love incarnate, he says, in the lives of many of his church people. "My people stood by me." He says that with deep gratitude. The usual accepted "scriptural grounds" for divorce did not enter into this particular situation; nor, in fact, in the others I interviewed.

The remarried minister commented:

> My people now see that my own life isn't all "put together," as the kids say. I'm struggling too. I have needs, failures, and sins. I think this is refreshing and helpful to people.
>
> But then I was faced with the decision—was I going to be content to live along the rest of my life? I felt that I just could not do that. The more I thought and prayed about it, the more convinced I became that if there is grounds for divorce—not necessarily the "scriptural grounds"—that there is grounds for remarriage, but then only in the Lord and directed by his will. I can't believe

that God would put a man in a state of limbo in that regard. I think that is an incomplete kind of view. It troubles me greatly that so much of the Christian world regards remarriage almost as the unpardonable sin.

Just because I had gotten a divorce did not mean that I still didn't feel an inner call from the Lord. I felt strongly that God still had his hand on me; he was still using me in the ministry. I couldn't get away from it. I knew I wanted to move on into the mainstream of Christianity, even more than what I had been in thus far in my Christian walk, and I had already been in the ministry thirteen years. But I did feel the need for a wife.

I believe right here is the proper place to interject what Jesus himself said on this subject—this need that does present itself to the divorced man and woman. In Matthew 19, where Jesus is having the discussion with the Pharisees with regard to divorce, the disciples said to Jesus that perhaps it would be better not to marry. His answer to them reveals the totality of his understanding of the human heart and body and our emotional makeup. Let us never forget that it was God who made the first man and then gave to him a woman because he saw that it was not good for man to be alone. Jesus said, "Not everyone can accept this statement" (about not marrying). "Only those whom God helps . . . but let anyone who can, accept my statement" (vs. 10–12).

The remarried pastor with whom I conversed about the problems thrown up by the Christian world to those who wish to remarry or, in fact, do, said:

I moved into a whole new phase of life with remarriage. I feel as if God gave me a new lease on life. Prior to the divorce I was almost destroyed as a person. What good would I have been to the Lord in that condition? But now I have a wife who really understands me as a person. God gave her to me, of that I am totally convinced. We have a ministry for the Lord together.

Another divorced, but as yet unremarried, pastor confessed that he fully intends to remarry. He referred to Jesus' answer to his disciples and said:

That includes me. I'm heterosexual. Women are very important to me. After all, they constitute more than 50 percent just in numbers alone in society. Let's face it. We men find great satisfaction in knowing women. For the first year after our divorce I didn't date; but now occasionally I do and find it very rewarding. This is, however, very much a matter of prayer with me before God. If he wants me to find the right woman and remarry, he will provide her for me in his time. Meanwhile, I am going to enjoy their company and conversation. Women are intelligent creatures, attractive, fun to be with, and I think God did a great thing when he made them.

The women whom I interviewed shared the same feelings with regard to men. "I need a husband," said one attractive blond.

I need the loving companionship of someone whom I can look up to and respect. I know this is biblical—we are to be subordinate and to submit and look up to our husbands. I didn't have that in my first marriage. I wanted it. But men have to earn our respect; they have to be worthy of it before we can honestly give it to them. I couldn't respect my husband. Our marriage failed for many reasons, and we both contributed to that failure. But I do want to be remarried, only this time it will be in God's time and his choice for me.

Another woman emphasized her strong beliefs in Ephesians 5, the verses dealing with the duties of the family and the husbands' and wives' relationship to each other before the Lord. There was a deep awareness among the divorced Christians whom I interviewed about what the Bible has to say regarding divorce and the proper marriage relationship as such that is insurance against the tragedy of divorce. I could sense that these Christians had not entered into divorce lightly.

Yes, God has given us perfect, flawless laws, and the marriage law is one of them. Jesus upheld God's laws; but I believe it can be said that when the law makes of men murderers, haters, and adulterers—even in one's heart, if not in actual life—didn't Jesus say that whosoever looketh upon a woman to lust after her hath committed adultery with her already in his heart (Matt. 5:28, *AV*)—then, like Jesus, to accomplish God's more perfect law of love, God will tolerate the setting aside of the law.

C. S. Lovett says, regarding this:

> Marriage, while it is high and holy and may well be one of man's highest institutions, does not exist for its own sake. Marriage is specifically designed to produce and accomplish something in men's lives. Little is gained by having two people co-exist for the sake of doing so, and it is when the higher goal of God in man is threatened that the marriage law may be set aside. Preserving rules for the sake of the rules themselves, has never been a penchant of the Lord. It is worth repeating that He is a Father, not a Lawyer. Marriage is good and holy, but when it works to defeat God's main purpose in man, divorce can become the better part, for it more nearly accomplishes God's will. By the same token, however, if divorce were discovered to produce the greater evil, then it would be outlawed by the same principle. . . .

When the Pharisees proposed the question of Moses'

institution of divorce in the wilderness, the whole issue of God's dealing with sinful man comes to view. It is revealed that the perfect law encounters difficulty when imposed upon sinful man, for instead of helping him, it becomes his executioner. Because of this God must employ a principle which takes man's failure into account. That principle, *God is willing to tolerate an evil which keeps his law from producing a greater evil*, is scripturally demonstrated in at least five distinct ways. . . .

The law was producing injustices, all worse than divorce itself. . . . God, in dealing with men under his Law, suffers divorce as a means of acknowledging man's failure; not as a means of acknowledging the Law's failure. The divorce statute was an accommodation to a world of sin. While God is holy, He is not unrealistic. The cross stands as supreme evidence of God's awareness that man is helpless under the Law, and that He is willing to make provision for those who are not able to measure up to its holy demands. The cross itself is the most challenging example of the toleration principle, for God willingly tolerated the murder of His Son to keep His own Law from sending us to hell![3]

Jesus has clearly shown that we disobey God's laws not only in actual deeds but also in the heart. It goes without saying that if we can break the laws from the heart, we should be obeying them from the heart as well. Outward obedience isn't all that is required. Heart obedience is also included. And God alone and his Son can see the heart. There are some of us who, having come to that recognition, finally reached the point where we sought divorce. We wanted to live as openly before the world as we were already living before the Lord. We had confessed to him our heart's disobedience; we had the assurance that he forgave.

So it is in the civil marriage ceremony that we are saying to the world that this is an inward union of two hearts; but wedding ceremonies per se are too often interpreted as marriage by God, when in actual fact this may not be the case at all. Two hands joined before a preacher or justice of the peace is no guarantee that two hearts have been joined by God. Sometimes recognition of this—and in the case of many of the divorced people whom I talked to this was true—comes later in life, sometimes it comes almost immediately after the marriage ceremony; and the couple hang in there thinking time will improve things. Sometimes the marriage does change—God is still in the miracle-working business—but when it does not change, then the outward act of divorce by a legal action is only a confirmation of the heart divorce that took place long before the parties appeared in court.

> There are many Christian homes that are spiritually divorced, yet there is no accompanying outward manifestation of it. They have not gone to the divorce court, but they are still divorced as far as God is concerned. They say, "I can't get a divorce, because I am a Christian. I don't believe in divorce." What they are really saying is, "I don't believe in *legal* and *civil* divorce." They do believe in divorce all right, because they have allowed themselves to be spiritually separated from their mates. They are already divorced from each other in the sight of God even though there is no human acknowledgment. If one is really concerned with obeying the Word of God, then it is obedience in the sight of God that is important, not that which appears acceptable in the eyes of the community.[4]

Lovett believes that without true heart union, people are living in a spiritually adulterous state and in clear violation of the seventh Commandment. His reasoning:

It's bound to be a shock when one considers that people living together with unjoined hearts are adulterers, but that's what the Word of God declares. It makes no difference to God whether or not a civil procedure of some kind has taken place. His records are not altered with the banging of an earthly judge's gavel.

More than one Christian, who has viciously pounced upon a divorced brother, is himself living in a state of spiritual adultery and just as guilty as far as God is concerned. The mask of propriety, while deceiving to the church family and the neighbors, makes no impression upon God.[5]

In any discussion of remarriage one must take into account what the Apostle Paul has to say on the subject. The seventh chapter of 1 Corinthians is often called the "Pauline Privilege." Again we must look at the background, the specific situation in which Paul's teaching is set forth. We find here that Paul reminds his hearers that "the time is short" (vs. 29). Paul knew that great persecution was to befall Christians. He, like other early Christians, was looking for the imminent return of Christ.

Paul has often been referred to as a woman-hater, mainly because of this chapter. I do not believe he was against women; elsewhere we hear him sending thank yous to the women who worked side by side with him in telling the "good news of the Gospel" to others. He calls them co-laborers.

But Paul's view led him to speak against marriage because of the difficult times they, as Christians, faced. With his strong conviction of the imminent second coming of Christ, Paul regarded marriage as unnecessary, and being single the better way to serve Christ. He expressed the wish that everyone could get along without marrying, just as he. But he admits that we are not all the same (vs. 7). He then adds that if you can't control yourselves, go ahead and marry. It is better to marry than to burn with lust (vs. 9). Marriage is God's remedy for lust; this Paul readily admits. He talks about divorce and separation, counseling in regard to various types of situations that may occur. In general, he says, marriage, by God's command, is for life. Paul does make a strong plea for those married to live in peace. He says, "For God wants His children to live in peace and harmony" (vs. 15).

In Ephesians 5, Paul also talks about the spiritual aspects of marriage. The goal of marriage is that the man and woman live in peace. If one's marriage is not bringing fulfillment, if there is great unpeace, then what? Not only can unpeace come when one is married to an unbeliever, as Paul talks about in verse 15; but there are other problem areas that produce lack of peace and harmony. Should a Christian continue to live under torment, in a form of slavery and bondage, under the yoke of a law that is destroying him or her as a person? Paul had found glorious liberty and freedom from the lofty provision of the law through Jesus Christ. He could say that the law of the Spirit of life in Christ Jesus had made him free from the law of sin and death. "For what the law could not do, in that it was weak through the flesh, God sending his own Son in the likeness of sinful flesh, and for sin, condemned sin in the flesh" (Rom. 8:2, 3).

Paul speaks of this newfound freedom. Thus it is as we take the whole counsel of God, as given through the Gospels and through Paul and other writers, that we recognize the cross is God's provision made for men under the law. There is no other way for sinners—divorced people, drunkards, gossips, backbiters, etc.—to escape the perfect law. There are no loopholes in the Bible large enough into which any of us can slide to justify our sinfulness.

Think on These Things

Those wishing to remarry are unwise to seek "escape" passages in the Bible. We all stand equally guilty before a Holy God and his perfect law. Let us cease trying to rationalize our way out of our situations, but let us rather accept what God has provided. God is not necessarily pleased with blind obedience to his law regarding marriage when we violate his laws in other ways. Let us not violate the heart of God but believe his Word.

"For God so loved the world, that he gave his only begotten Son, that whosoever [insert your own name here if you have accepted Christ into your heart] believeth in him should not perish, but have everlasting life" (John 3:16, *AV*).

If I understand God's Word correctly, that "whosoever" provision is for *all* sinners who come to him believing and accepting what he has done—yes, even divorced and remarried Christians.

13

Are There Any Deterrents to Divorce?

There is a shrinking minority in the world today, particularly in the United States, of the happily married. When a couple marry, matrimony appears on the horizon of life as an oasis, offering joy and fulfillment; but as this book has pointed out, many marriages turn out to be mirages, offering nothing but heartache and disappointment.

Matrimony has been defined in many ways, but the person who said marriage is a high sea for which no compass has yet been invented has come up with a fairly accurate definition. It's been said that the old ship of matrimony that God launched in the Garden of Eden has been caught in a cyclone of change. Of every dozen wedded couples (according to studies by John Cuber and Peggy Harroff), four will jump overboard, six will stay lashed on deck by utilitarian interests—children, career, family, church, etc.—without joy or love, and only two will enjoy what Dr. Joyce Brothers calls "total" marriages where they will share a lifetime of happiness. It is alarming and tragic to realize that so many marriages which begin happily at the altar end up on the rocks.

"Divorce has become as much an institution as marriage itself," states Herbert A. Otto, a fellow of the American Association of Marriage Counselors. He has also raised the question, "Has monogamy failed?"

The French biographer André Maurois has stated succinctly, "Marriage is an edifice that has to be rebuilt every day." It would appear that many couples are busy razing their marriages rather than enjoying and building them. What is cracking the structure of marriage?

It is a well-known fact that in the fall of ancient Rome, as deduced from the writing of noted historians, the breakdown of the family and the rapid increase of divorce was at the top of the list of contributing factors. Those Christian couples who fail to achieve marital harmony and end up as divorce statistics must share in the responsibility of what happens to *this* country as a result of the ascending divorce rate. What can be done about this ascending rate that is, in reality, an ugly downward spiral? What, specifically, can Christians do to deter divorce among their own ranks and, hopefully, to influence and help others so that this rate can decline?

There are no pat answers, contrary to what many books, magazine articles, counselors, and pastors may espouse. There are times, when I read and hear comments and listen to sermons on the subject, that I want to stand up and shout that it isn't that simple. I want to say, "You haven't been there—you aren't divorced—your nice formulas, your reasoning and advice, well meant as they are, are just too pat. Some of this may work for some and if so, great, keep it up; but qualify your statements, make allowances for the fact that we don't all fit into the same mold. What works for some couples, just may not work for others."

All kinds of books have been and are being written on the subject of marriage. The titles are thought-provoking, and the authors are, for the most part, credible; the publishers are reputable. I've quoted from them dozens of times. I'll continue to do so. I'm not going to try and improve upon what has already been so well written by many who are recognized experts. I do recommend that such books be read and digested. Absorb what you can, diligently apply their suggestions to your own experience, and consciously strive to do what they say—really work at it. At the top of my recommended reading list would be the Bible in as many fine paraphrases and translations as you can afford. Read and compare the references given in this book; and, in particular, read and reread Eph. 5:21–33.

Are there any deterrents to divorce, things that can be done or said as preventive measures which actual victims of divorce themselves recommend? Indeed there are. Many of these things are discussed in the types of books I have already alluded to, but let's listen to them from the lips and experiences of those Christians who've been there, those for whom the word "divorce" is more than an ugly word—a reality.

Everyone, it seems, agrees with the familiar maxim that says that success in marriage is more than marrying the right person, it is *being* the right person. A man and a woman are intent on being something very special to each other before marriage, and they work at it all through their courtship days. A very beautiful remarried woman in her mid-forties said to me with a glow in her eyes, "My husband has never stopped courting me." This wise husband was intent on *being* to his wife exactly what he was to her before he wooed and won her. She, in turn, had eyes only for him. Both had been divorced, and this was, as the popular song says, "the second time around." Taped to the mirror in their bedroom I saw a little note that read: "I love you bushels and bushels." It was signed by her husband, and is typical of the small things that go into *being* the right person in marriage.

Contrast that kind of an attitude to the husband who habitually tongue-lashes his wife, who verbally abuses her to the point where she is so demeaned she is almost destroyed. Would he have done that to her and won her affection before they were married? Or the same thing can happen with a woman tearing down her man's ego to inflate her own self-image. It can only result in the death of love. "Who wants to be run over by his wife's tongue every time he steps in the door?" one man questioned.

Said a very dignified gentleman,

I was good for one thing; to be a puppet on a string for my wife. She didn't want a husband, she wanted a slave to cater to her every whim. She was happy only when I was pampering her. Did I get that kind of treatment from her? Not on your life! She feigned illnesses of all kinds to hold me, when all she would have needed to do was stop thinking only of herself.

The list of things both men and women related to me as being what they considered wrong treatment added up to a giant-sized, nauseating assault on human dignity. I do not know what kind of treatment this man's wife actually was giving him, nor whether what he was saying was an exaggeration or the complete truth. But these were Christian men and women whom I interviewed, individuals for whom the word "divorce" was just as distasteful as it is to you. The last thing in the world that any of them wanted was for their marriage to end up in the casualty column of the daily paper under the heading *Divorced.*

Conflict is inevitable between two normal beings; but I am convinced that by God's grace two mature people can face their areas of conflict, discuss them, and, by obeying the injunctions of God's Word, resolve them. But it takes two who are willing to do this, two working together as one. Both a Christian psychologist and a minister who was a divorce victim emphasized the fact that it takes concentrated effort by both the husband and wife in order to put a marriage back together that has disintegrated. "No matter how hard a single individual works, if there isn't an almost equivalent of that work by the other marriage partner, the marriage is doomed," said the pastor.

If two things are to stick together, they must have an adhesive. Just so in marriage, if two persons are to be "one," they must have an adhesive. Christians know that "adhesive" is to be God. Marriage to be ideal is a triangular relationship—the triangle formed by God, the husband, and the wife. In that triangular relationship, there is one manual on human behavior that surpasses every other book or manual on the market. Of course that is the Bible. When used rightly by marriage partners, the Bible can turn chaos into peace and harmony. But it takes two mature people willing to face their areas of conflict, willing to admit their own weaknesses and then to discuss these things, and, by obeying the injunctions of God's Word, work to resolve them.

Notice that word "mature." Such maturity is not altogether related to chronological calendar years. It has more to do with the growing up that comes in not insisting on one's own way. It is making a determined, unselfish effort to understand your mate's needs and temperament; it has a lot to do with accepting one's mate at face value.

Such acceptance means you don't persist in trying to "change" your partner. "My husband constantly tried to 'change' me," said one woman. "He simply would not accept me as I was. All I ever heard was, 'You've got to change, you've got to change.' I was good enough for him before he married me," she reasoned, "why couldn't he accept me that way after we married. I hadn't changed for the worse, to my knowledge," she stated. This woman's psychologist confirmed that all the husband talked about when he came for counseling sessions was, "———has to change," and then he proceeded to spell out every area in which he felt his wife needed changing. When it was suggested that perhaps there should be some changing on the part of both of them, he became irate. The psychologist could only advise divorce.

Such a selfish attitude is not conducive to an honest exchange of communication. Two such individuals constantly at each other's throat cannot read the Bible and pray together as a result. This is what is happening in many Christian homes. Stubbornness, pride, selfishness, immaturity—Jesus called it hardness of heart. But the recognition must come to the Christian church that this problem does exist; it is another side of divorce not discussed in the Bible under the subject of divorce itself.

It is a recognized fact that many marriages break down at this very point—where one or another of the marriage partners is so hung up on this idea of "change" that nothing and no one can get through to them. Only by a miracle of God does this happen; when that miracle doesn't occur, love is killed, never to be rekindled again. Constant criticism and suggesting of changes only increases resistance and breaks down communication. Prodding and pushing decreases love, understanding, and acceptance.

Let it not be said, however, that sometimes changes are not necessary, or that this writer doesn't recognize this. Very often changes are necessary. But where does one begin to try to help one's mate to recognize this for herself or himself without alienating them? The place to begin is with yourself. The first help a couple can actually give each other is acceptance. Genuine acceptance. Fake acceptance will not do; it will be recognized for what it is—subterfuge. Mutual acceptance—as between equals—is necessary.

Gibson Winter, in his book *Love and Conflict*, says:

> Acceptance in marriage is the power to love someone and receive him in the very moment that we realize how far he [or she] falls short of our hopes. It is love between two people who see clearly that they do not measure up to one another's dreams. Acceptance is loving the real person to whom one is married. Acceptance is giving up dreams for reality.

We must begin with ourselves—begin by being the kind of changed person, in every way you know, that you would like your wife or husband to become. Yes, success in marriage is more than marrying the right person; it is *being* the right person.

141

How can marital partners achieve unity? Paul gives a pattern for this in Phil. 2:1-8. But how many couples apply this to marriage? Few, I fear. He says: "Is there any such thing as Christians cheering each other up? Do you love me enough to want to help me? Does it mean anything to you that we are brothers in the Lord, sharing the same Spirit? Are your hearts tender and sympathetic at all? Then make me truly happy by loving each other and agreeing whole-heartedly with each other, working together with one heart and mind and purpose. Don't be selfish; don't live to make a good impression on others. Be humble, thinking of others as better than yourself. Don't just think about your own affairs, but be interested in others, too, and in what they are doing. Your attitude should be the kind that was shown us by Jesus Christ, who, though he was God, did not demand and cling to his rights as God, but laid aside his mighty power and glory, taking the disguise of a slave and becoming like men. And he humbled himself even further, going so far as actually to die a criminal's death on a cross."

Paul goes on to say that God rewarded his Son for this by raising him up to the heights of heaven. I believe God would do the same for married couples today who would follow Jesus' example and habitually make this the pattern of their every word and deed. Paul begs his readers to stay away from arguing and complaining and to live as children of God in this dark world which is so full of people who are crooked and stubborn (vs. 14, 15).

If you want your marriage partner to treat you with consideration and thoughtfulness, then be mature enough by God's grace to treat him or her that way. Too many Christians act as though injunctions in the Bible regarding the treatment of others are to be applied to everyone else in the Christian world with the exception of their respective mates! We use our tongues to cut each other down to size; we are unforgiving, jealous, temperamental; we forget to show the little kindnesses and courtesies that are so important (little things do mean a lot); tenderness is an almost forgotten act between husbands and wives; and we do (or fail to do) and say all sorts of things that we would never dream of doing or saying to a casual acquaintance, neighbor, or fellow Christian. And then we wonder why our marriages turn sour!

In a good marriage—a peaceful, harmonious relationship—you do not do anything from a sense of duty but from a sense of pleasure in making a happy environment for the person with whom you are sharing your life. There must be a deep caring for each other, a desire to please your mate, putting his wishes before your own.

The Bible says that no man may divorce what God has joined together (Matt. 19:6). After talking with many individuals, I am led to believe that many Christians never consulted God regarding their life partner. What might well be considered the most important step an individual makes—outside of the step that one takes in accepting Christ—is made without taking God's will into account, without honestly calling upon him for clear direction. I must confess that in my own case this was true, and most of the divorced Christians with whom I conversed made this confession. We were young, immature, and unwise. Some of us disregarded the counsel of our elders; and most of us did not seek God's counsel. Those of us who were guilty of this were, for the most part, young in the faith as well as young in years. God did not do the joining. On the basis of what the Scripture says regarding what God hath joined together, if we say we do not believe in divorce then we are forced to say that God has joined every couple who has ever been married. That is, of course, a position that is untenable through and through. We cannot regard every marriage as the joining of a man and a woman by God. The church and pastor marrying the couple assumes that the union it is celebrating is in accordance with the will of God; but no church by its blessing can transform unions which are entered into lightly and irresponsibly and make the marriages such as God would ideally have them to be.

The important point here, however, is that our children and future generations be taught that if they want God-blessed marriages and happiness in their marital state, then they must earnestly seek God's guidance as to the selection of a life partner. As mature Christians who have come to know the importance of seeking God's will, we know we must be ready to wait upon him for the answers; but many young people have not learned this. Many individuals acknowledged that they rushed into marriage totally unprepared for the responsibilities that faced them. When the first glow of the honeymoon had rubbed off and they faced reality, they were disillusioned and unable to cope. They struggled along for years experiencing highs and lows in their marriage, never resolving their problems, living in constant conflict, their homes a battlefield.

We must remember that God wants happiness for his children. God wants the best for us and is prepared to give it. In cases of Christians divorcing each other, we are seeing many instances of individuals who ran ahead of God. David the psalmist sought God's best. When confronted with life's choices he pondered and said, "Lord, I want Your blessings with all my heart. Be merciful just as You promised. I thought about the wrong direction I was headed. I turned around and came running to You, Lord" (Ps. 119:58–60).

David learned that those who search for God's will and then do it are happy. Read Psalm 119. It should be the prayer of everyone.

We must know, however, that we do not come to God merely seeking his advice; we are to come seeking his will. Following his will may cost us something but in the final analysis will bring the greatest rewards. In regard to seeking one's life partner, it may mean giving up someone whom we thought we dearly loved. This is a choice that many are not prepared to make. They will not accept the well-meant advice of others; they do not look into God's Word, nor do they heed their own inner conscience sending up warning signals. These are things divorced individuals whom I talked to admitted.

Can divorce be avoided? Yes, by seeking God's clear will at the outset of one's relationship with a member of the opposite sex. Some men "take a wife" while others "receive a wife" as God's gift. God has given us the example of how he will do this in his Word. God gave Eve to Adam as a helpmeet. When Eve was created, God brought her to Adam. God can bring the right man and the right woman into our lives. One twice-married man believes the answer to the American divorce problem is that "we all should marry our second wives first!" In God's perfect timing this could have happened the first time around if those of us who married without seeking his will would only have done this and then waited on God to give us that person. When this is done, we can have the assurance that our marriages can become highways to fulfillment and true happiness, rather than dead ends of bitterness, despair, and divorce.

Another area frequently mentioned by divorced individuals, which I have already alluded to, is this matter of marrying too young. I have frequently made the comment that the years of single bliss are very, very few in comparison to the years of marriage. Diapers, dishes, and drudgery—the three Ds that are the downfall of many marriages—are more than words beginning with D. They are a reality, and unless the woman is prepared for this and satisfied with her "single fling," she had better not settle into the marriage role. This role for women is changing, but there are some matters relating to what is expected of a wife and mother that will never change.

Today many couples are flaunting tradition in the face and are cohabiting, believing this to be a deterrent to divorce. Is such living together to be considered a dress rehearsal for marriage? The new, open way to look at marriage, with advocates among scholars as well as women's liberationists, says that trial marriages will stem the soaring divorce rate. Marital unhappiness is considered a social problem; some say a social crisis. The traditional marriage, with its emphasis on roles and obligations, it is said, forces women into a dependent, subordinate position and restricts the human development of both sexes. The Christian world, however, cannot accept anything other than what the Bible lays down regarding marriage. Even though divorce does exist among the ranks of Christians, and sadly, is growing, it does not mean divorced Christians are compromising their views. God has given the ideal and nowhere does he sanction trial marriage, or, if we are to put it bluntly, "shacking up."

Social mores are loosening and changing, options for women are increasing, and the distractions and tensions of an ever more complex world are robbing wedlock of many formerly taken-for-granted safeguards. Couples are confronted with multiplied temptations. Today many are ready to ring the deathknell over wedlock, looking, as they do, with concern at the mounting divorce rate, the growing tendency to disregard marriage vows, and the tendency to form households of unmarried couples. The result is a serious crisis for the institution of marriage, which, more than any other, has been the breeder and preserver of human progress. Those of us who are divorced, as much as those who are not divorced, cannot help but view what we see happening with concern. It is right to be concerned but wrong to despair. God gave the institution of marriage for man's highest good; those of us who have failed but who certainly do not want to fail again are especially anxious to do what we can to help others step into right marriage relationships and work to stay there.

One woman writing to "Dear Abby" stated that twenty

years ago she decided to resign herself to her unhappy marriage state. "I made the best of a marriage with a dull, unresponsive husband, and I suppressed everything I felt inside, and even convinced myself that I was in control and was doing the right thing," she stated. She went on to explain that now she was forty-five; her children were grown and gone; and all the frustrations she'd suppressed for years have suddenly broken through. She recognizes now that she'd done not only herself but her husband a great injustice, and that they had both been cheated. She concluded by stating, "I don't know yet how this will turn out, but the realization that I've compromised my life away is almost unbearable . . . right now I'm dealing and facing my inner feelings honestly. And dear God," she wrote, "how it hurts!"

One wonders how many men and women identified with that woman. How can this be avoided? If we can't undo the past and live our own lives over, we can surely make a more determined effort to pass on to our children and others what we have learned.

I would urge upon young people the necessity of developing priorities early in life. Begin by asking these important questions: (1) What do I want to achieve in my life? (2) How can I best go about working to accomplish this? (3) What qualities do I want in the person I hope to marry?

I would urge young people not to be in too much of a hurry to get married. Relax. Enjoy many friendships with members of the opposite sex along the way. The more such friendships you cultivate, the better able you will be, as you mature in your thinking, to sort out feelings and impressions. Learn to keep your emotions in check as you move along the way. That, I know, is a big order. How does a person with developing sensitivities keep his or her emotions in check? Go slow! And don't place yourself in any kind of situation where things can get out of hand. Dating has been described as "a young person's experiment with the future." It's a time to discover your own strengths and weaknesses and similar traits of character in those with whom you date. Work to develop emotional balance. Fix in your mind a definite way of behavior for yourself and also what you expect from the one whom you are dating. Then determine, with God's help, to act accordingly. Believe me, if I had fixed in my mind more definite priorities, if I had outlined specific goals for the future—the kind of man I really needed and wanted—and sought God's leading, and if I had set my eyes fixed on achieving these priorities, I, like many others, would not today be a divorce statistic.

Let me reemphasize that the best way to prevent a marriage mistake is to seek God's will, establish values, life styles, and goals consistent with what the Bible indicates as being right and good, and think long and hard before saying yes to a proposal of marriage. The better you know yourself—and God can help you come to grips with the real you—the better you will be able to assess whether someone else can fill those needs. Don't get too romantically involved too early; your chemical reaction to a member of the opposite sex, while it may indicate love, is not necessarily so. There's more to marriage than sex and making love in or out of bed.

Immaturity is one of the greatest factors contributing to marriage failure—young people getting married when they really aren't even grown-up yet, whose entire value system often changes as late as twenty-five years or older. One minister stated that in the hundreds of cases that have come to his attention of broken marriages, two factors stand out as major causes: sex ignorance and marriage prior to age twenty. From what I could gather in my interviews and research, it is felt the best age for a man to marry is around twenty-four to twenty-six; and the best age for a girl is between twenty-three and twenty-five. It is also felt that when the man is older than the woman, the chances for happiness are better. There's something about being able to look up to and respect someone who stands above you in years that has a healthy effect upon a woman.

I cringe when I hear comments made that people today are entering into marriage with the idea that if it doesn't work out they can always get a divorce. This is rarely the case; it is more talk than reality! I find it difficult to believe that idealistic young couples embarking upon the sea of matrimony really regard marriage that way. Perhaps I am the one who is unrealistic. I did not enter my marriage that way; every woman I've talked to—divorced or married—did not think that way; and the young girls I've talked to do not feel that way. I really believe there is a basic goodness about people, and they genuinely want their marriages to survive. One couple, married sixty-nine years, said, "We think our marriage lasted because we believed marriage was permanent, forever. So we worked hard to solve our problems. We never thought about running away from them."

The husband in that marriage said, "We've been fighting about everything under the sun ever since we got married. I've wanted to knock her head off a few times," he said, chuckling at her glare. "And anybody who thinks you can stay married very long to the same woman without fighting is either an idiot or a liar. But I wouldn't change a thing if I could call back the years. We've been happy together."

How do you attain to such happiness? Certainly not by holding grudges and being unwilling to forgive and forget. Certainly not by refusing to share responsibilities regarding the home and children. Certainly not by arguing about money and failing to come to some basic agreement regarding finances and then working at this together. "Togetherness," it seems, is a clue.

THINK ON THESE THINGS

Of the many fine books which have been written on the subject of how to attain marital happiness, one of the best is

Tim LaHaye's *How to Be Happy Though Married*.[1] The reader is well-advised to read this excellent volume. In this book, the author gives six keys to marital happiness. Think on these: Maturity; Submission; Love; Communication; Prayer; and Christ.

> Let nothing be done through strife or vainglory; but in lowliness of mind let each esteem other better than themselves. Look not every man on his own things, but every man also on the things of others (Phil. 2:3–4, *AV*).

14
Togetherness

Divorce is only the visible part of an iceberg, just a symptom of a deeper trouble in American family life. What is going on in American family life is war in the living room, a struggle to cope with the basic technological and social assault of change.[1]

But oftentimes the war in the living room had its start in the bedroom. Sex was not intended to be a one-night affair; but many couples act that way. Either may be the offending partner in the battle of sex. "My husband treats me with contempt all day long; yet at bedtime everything's supposed to be so great, and I'm to turn on as easily as an electric light. Forget him." She was headed for the divorce mill.

Or it may go like this:

All she wanted from me was sex and money. She was always complaining—too sick to clean the house; too sick to cook the meals. Our house was considered a showplace—I couldn't even put my head back on an upholstered chair or the couch—"You'll get grease on it." She insisted I turn my paycheck over to her, and she doled out my weekly allowance. Yet when we got into bed at night, all she wanted was for me to fuss over her, to make passionate love, tell her how beautiful she was, how desirable, how she turned me on, and all the rest. What did she do to precipitate a desire on my part for lovemaking? Not one thing.

The complaints went on like that ad infinitum from both men and women. The act of sex in its highest and most beautiful form comes as a result of the intercourse of loving words, acts, and deeds that have gone on all day between a husband and a wife. Two become one in true intimacy when the love relationship extends throughout each day, on into the next day, and on and on and on. This can only happen when a man and a woman are working at their marriage together.

The Bible speaks of adultery in marriage, which I've already discussed. There are other ways in which marriage partners are adulterating their relationship. There is distrust for instance. A couple who have been married for seventy-three years believes that the success of their marriage lies in their mutual trust. Jealousy is a consuming fire, the Bible warns, and for good reason. "I never got jealous," the ninety-two-year-old wife in this marriage stated. "That's the quickest way to lose your husband, you know. Not trust him. You just have to leave your man alone and know that he loves you."

The general consensus seems to be that if a man or woman's married life is as it should be, then he or she shouldn't have a constant and insatiable desire to seek out the company of another man or woman. But to what degree is infidelity contributing to divorce among Christians? One dislikes to even bring up that subject in a book directed to Christians. Ideally the problem shouldn't exist; but the problem does exist, no use denying it.

Dr. Shirley Firman, a sociologist and author of a book on marriage problems, says that her studies confirm the fact that men—especially married men—are, as a race, infinitely more secretive and devious than women give them credit for. In one study she conducted, she became concerned with the fact that 240 out of 400 men interviewed claimed they had had some form of extramarital relationship—often what they considered "pretty harmless"—and in less than 10 percent of the cases did the wife ever learn anything about it.[2]

As Christians we cannot consider extramarital relations "pretty harmless," and most psychologists and counselors will agree that the act of coitus does something to a man and woman at the very deepest level of their inner being that can never be undone. No matter how casual the sex contact, what the Bible says still remains as absolute fact: "Do you know that if a man joins himself to a prostitute she becomes a part of him and he becomes a part of her? For God tells us in the Scripture that in his sight the two become one person" (1 Cor. 6:16).

The effects of sex are permanent. They sear one's memory; what has happened remains, even though it may be pushed into one's subconscious. The Bible gives many illustrations to show the damaging effects of playing with sex. Generally we think of David and Bathsheba, but there are others whose affairs resulted in great heartache not only to themselves but to the nation and those whose lives touched theirs in one way or another.

Those who shared their confidences with me admitted, however, that there is no satisfying sexual relationship apart from the permanency of marriage. There is mistrust and jealousy. "If she would give herself to me and be disloyal to her husband, how can I be certain she isn't giving herself to others," is the line of reasoning. Women reasoned the same way. There is an inner something built into us that craves the security that comes from knowing we belong to someone whom we can trust.

There is no such guarantee of security where there has been infidelity. It plagues the guilty partner for the rest of his or her life and haunts the one offended. David Augsburger explains it like this:

Any person who plays with sex fragments his own soul. Inner disintegration sets in; he is torn and divided. Anxiety and guilt set in, or if he can cleverly silence that, it wreaks its punishment in boredom and alienation

153

from others, and results in the inability to love, to give genuine devotion to another. It incapacitates anyone from experiencing genuine loyalty, security, fidelity, and unity in life and love.

But sex rightly used, faithfully kept, and unselfishly shared within marriage brings a high and holy unity between two personalities. Two become one in true intimacy.

Intimacy in open honesty before each other and before God. This is the key to it all.[3]

When the Bible says "Honor your marriage and its vows and be pure, for God will surely punish all those who are immoral or commit adultery" (Heb. 13:4), it means just that. The toll in emotional havoc that is wrought by infidelity is unbelievably heartbreaking. Ask the man or woman who's been there.

Sociologists speak of the present "new morality" (which is as old as history) as causing a special sort of insecurity and hurt. Sex outside of marriage exacts a high price in emotional instability. The hurt is in the soul.

Someone wrote to Billy Graham's "My Answer" column in the paper wanting to know if two people who are practically engaged, couldn't have sex before marriage. They questioned if God wouldn't understand this expression of love by reasoning that, after all, is there any good reason for postponing a relationship that seems so right?

The answer stated in part that God knows all about love, since he created it in the first place. But don't ask God to wink at, much less endorse, a violation of his creative plan. In both the Old and New Testaments, the sexual relationship is looked upon as natural and wholesome, but always as a part of marriage. When one has sex outside of marriage, there's no protection against suspicion and distrust. It's an adventure all right, but a jaded one in a potentially poisonous atmosphere that offers no destination.

Billy Graham cautioned readers not to get caught in the tragedy of living only at the physical level, where you function on the basis of promiscuous performance. God can give sex a spiritual dimension and surround it with principled purpose. Use the will that God gave you and reserve sex for the only setting where it belongs—marriage.[4]

But what about those marriages where infidelity has occurred? Marital unfaithfulness is considered the scriptural grounds for divorce; however, unfaithfulness need not automatically end a marriage. There can be repentance, forgiveness, and restoration. But the "offended party," the one who takes the "offender" back, must make certain he or she is able to not only forgive, but forget. Forgetting is involved in forgiving.

Can there be real forgiveness without forgetting? God, in speaking through the prophet Isaiah, gave us this pattern for forgetting forgiveness. He said, "I, yes, I alone am he who blots away your sins for my own sake and will never think of them again" (Isa. 43:25).

The memories of the pain of another's misdeed may still exist; it takes time to forget, but if there is a supreme desire to forget, God can take care of that. Where there is an unwillingness or an inability to forget, the forgiveness is incomplete and the marriage will suffer. Regardless of how many times you may say to someone who has wronged you, "I forgive you," if you have not forgotten, then you have never really forgiven. If you find it necessary to remind that one, whether frequently or infrequently, of their betrayal, of their unfaithfulness, their untrustworthiness, then you have not forgiven him or her. God says, "I will remember your sins no more," and he is our pattern.

It is almost always necessary to seek professional help in such instances of unfaithfulness. But if the "offended party" cannot accept the professional counsel and does not work with his or her mate to rebuild the marriage relationship, but rather keeps on referring to it, throwing it in the other's face, then it would be far better to dissolve the marriage. On the basis of the conversations I have had with individuals involved in such situations, I am forced to conclude that unless there is a complete resurrender of both parties to each other and God, then it would be far better for everyone concerned for that marriage to terminate.

Jealousy, distrust, possessiveness—these are fatal to a happy marriage. A woman wrote a letter to Ann Landers in which she told of her husband's unfaithfulness. She didn't want a separation or a divorce. Her main concern was that her husband might be discovered by the town busybodies and it would ruin his reputation and possibly jeopardize his position with the company. She thought she would go to the president of the firm and ask him to break it up. Her reason? "To prevent a possible scandal."

Ann Landers replied: "Interesting that you are concerned about being 'betrayed,' yet you do not view your plan to tell on your husband as a betrayal of *him*. My advice is to stay away from the president and talk to your husband."

I believe we have to confront the question of "betrayal" in such cases as this. Often the "offended party" insists on revealing the facts concerning his or her "betrayal" to friends, business associates and family members. How sad! If, in order to hold onto one's mate, one has to resort to such techniques, how much wiser it would be to end the pretense, making it possible for a new life to be rebuilt for each one in that kind of a tangled situation.

What is it that leads to infidelity? "I honestly did not love my mate," said one individual. He went on:

> I was constantly seeking for that certain type of love which I know exists among some couples. I really wanted this. I am a Christian; I do love the Lord. He has filled that other certain vacuum in my life; but he has made me a very sexual being, and I just didn't receive from my mate that which I needed to satisfy that

longing. It wasn't just sexual—my mate wasn't all that bad in that regard—it was much deeper, much greater than that.

Another person shared:

My mate wouldn't do anything with me. I had to do and go to everything alone. There was no togetherness. She literally forced me into seeking companionship with someone else by refusing to share with me that in which I had to participate. She was extremely jealous and possessive. My ego needed bolstering after being torn down so constantly by her. The first time I was unfaithful she told everyone. You can imagine what this did to my standing among our friends and my co-workers—how extremely difficult this made it for me. I'm not excusing myself, but it seems to me if she loved me as much as was claimed, she would have done everything possible to stand by me with love and would have shielded this from others; instead, she used it to gain sympathy and attention for herself. From that time on our marriage was a marriage in name only. My infidelity was held over my head constantly both by my partner and at work, where I was frequently reminded not to associate with members of the opposite sex because I was too "vulnerable." I only stayed on at that job because I felt it was a God-given responsibility, an opportunity for me to use the gifts God had entrusted to me.

Christianity Today in its "Minister's Workshop" section carried an enlightening article by Henry Wildeboer on "Rebuilding Marital Fidelity," in which he states:

Explosive love relationships develop rather readily in our society . . . but sooner or later the marriage partner begins to sense that something is going on. Eventually the problem is exposed and major decisions have to be made. . . . The offended partner will, naturally, be deeply hurt. He or she may at first think divorce is the only solution. . . . A better solution is to forgive the offender and rebuild the marriage.

To begin the restoration, the hurt partner needs time to express his pain, bitterness, anger, hostility, or sorrow. Eventually, however, he must face the hard but necessary question, "What have I done that contributed to this situation?" Because the extramarital relationship often supplies what the marriage lacks, the answer is frequently one or more sins of omission, such as taking the other for granted, neglect, failing to provide reassurance, negligence in expressing appreciation, or failure to be attractive, accessible, approachable. . . .

When the offended partner realizes his own shortcomings and their contribution to the breakdown, he can, with God's help, begin to forgive the offender and rebuild trust. Although man's forgiveness is—like all else that he does—imperfect, both partners need to be willing to forgive as totally as they can. As divine forgiveness depends not on man's feeling forgiven but on God's declaration of forgiveness, to be accepted on the basis of his Word, so each of the partners must declare forgiveness of the other and then accept the other's forgiveness on the basis of his word. He must also learn to forgive himself, something that is often harder than forgiving the other person. . . .

The offending partner must break a deep emotional attachment in order to rebuild his marriage. He has learned to depend—wrongly so, to be sure—upon someone else to fulfill various important needs, and the required break will probably bring extreme pain and turmoil. The offended partner can help by trying—

despite his own anguish—to understand the painful "withdrawal" that accompanies his spouse's redirection of loyalty and dependence. More than anything else, both partners need someone with whom to share their burdens, and there is no better way to rebuild a marriage relationship than to begin again to lean on each other. Sharing the heavy burden helps redirect attachment to its proper object. To remove the illegitimate relationship without replacing it could lead to the fate of the man (in the Bible) who was cleansed but not refilled: seven worse demons came in and took over. The offended one may need help to resume his place as the needed one.

Both partners will need to renew their spiritual commitment. They must cultivate their love for Christ. For the offended one, that love will salve the wounds and help cleanse away the anger. The offender needs it to cleanse away the sin and the guilt. Both must appropriate the Holy Spirit's power: one will need it to stay mind and tongue in forgetfulness; the other will need it to maintain faithfulness. Both need the fruit of his presence: love.

The partners will need to renew their commitment to each other, not only in an emotional way but with a declaration—and deeds to fit the words. They will have to say to each other what, if they are Christians, they have already said to God: "I belong to you heart, soul, mind, and strength. I will do all I can to be faithful to you." Then they must practice loving each other. They must give as much of themselves as they are able to give—and want and work to give much more.

If a strong desire to give can be established, the marriage can be rebuilt, even from a very painful past. And the new relationship can be stronger than husband and wife have ever experienced before. Such a happy ending requires of both the strong desire to save the marriage and the maturity and flexibility to face their individual contributions to the breakdown. A minister's wise counsel, pointing them to God's example of love and forgiveness, may be the cornerstone of their new life together.[5]

One of the divorced ministers mentioned elsewhere in this book emphasized the necessity for husbands and wives to have a mutuality of faith and a mutuality of interests. In regard to the mutuality of faith, he stated:

Each one of us needs a partner to whom he can talk in depth about his faith—belief in God and love for Christ. I insisted upon family devotions in our home and know this was most significant in holding our family together for over thirty years. If we would not have had that mutuality of faith, I am certain the marriage would have disintegrated years earlier. I would say that husbands and wives who pray together have a much better chance of staying together. You can't pray heart and soul for your wife, or she for you, and not have God move in a mysterious way to strengthen and sustain your relationship.

Those Christians who have divorced would have to admit that failure at this point in their relationship contributed to the eventual divorce. Many such couples, however, would say—and it is true—that you cannot get down on your knees together and pray when one of you is mad at the other and unwilling to talk the situation over.

In regard to mutuality of interest, the before-mentioned divorced minister stated:

Mutual interests are terribly impor.ant for the success of a marriage. If there are things you enjoy doing together, it's cement that helps to bind your relationship. I don't think a marriage hardly ever comes apart in one shot; it begins to kind of strain at the seams and then split a little year by year. And, in particular, when a husband and a wife are not sharing in mutual interests, they drift farther and farther apart. It is very difficult for a marriage to last when there is no mutuality of interests and each partner is going off in different directions. I have seen it happen too often, and the marriage shreds very quickly.

If you've got mutuality of faith and mutuality of interests, I am convinced you've got a marriage that won't end up in divorce. In fact, I really don't know what could deteriorate in a marriage if you had that. If you wanted to do things together, and your faith was binding you to one another where you were practicing forgiveness and understanding with good communication, then you'd have a beautiful marriage. Love, affection, and the right sexual relationship will follow in a marriage if it's built on mutuality of faith and mutuality of interests.

The importance of mutuality of interests was borne out in discussions with several other divorced individuals. One person shared how his wife resented an interest that had been a mutually satisfying thing between them before marriage; as the years progressed, she became resentful and jealous of the very thing that drew them together to begin with. Among other things it became their livelihood, and it was a practical impossibility to leave. She would not participate in nor encourage him in this activity, and made it very difficult, even forcing him to lose several responsible jobs because of her resentment.

A woman related her keen disappointment that eventually resulted in a hurt so deep it drove a wedge between her and her husband; her husband would not support her in an endeavor that provided not only an extra income that they needed but was something she could not neglect. She was careful to guard against this superseding her interests in her husband, their business, and their children, yet she yearned for his support and encouragement. All she wanted was for him to show some pride in her as his wife, but it was not forthcoming.

Couples who do not work at this thing called "togetherness" will find themselves eventually with a sick marriage. It is difficult to understand how two people who could not bear to be apart for very long in their courtship days, who wanted to do everything together, can drift so far apart after marriage. Dr. Lindsay Curtis, a marriage counselor, often hands his clients a calling card that lists some of the warning signals of a sick marriage. The list reads like this:

Couples begin to think in terms of "I" instead of "We."
They fail to compliment each other, or to express love.
They fail to sense and meet each other's needs.
They stop praying together.

Dr. Curtis adds, "Prayer seems naive to a lot of people these days, but it's always been one of my favorite prescriptions for an ailing marriage."

Praying with and for each other helps build communication and opens the heart to being changed by God into the kind of person who can make a marriage work.

The Bible cautions that we are not to be unequally yoked with unbelievers. "Don't be teamed with those who do not love the Lord, for what do the people of God have in common with the people of sin? How can light live with darkness? And what harmony can there be between Christ and the devil? How can a Christian be a partner with one who doesn't believe?" (2 Cor. 6:14, 15).

Dr. David A. Hubbard, theologian, states that "When life is radically Christian, when faith really works, the will of God becomes our standard no matter what the social patterns around us may be." He believes that at the heart of God's program for our lives is a stable home. He cites 1 Thess. 4:3, where the Apostle Paul hits these subjects head on urging that each one take a wife for himself in holiness and honor, not in the passion of lust like heathen who do not know God. "Christian marriage is to have an entirely different style from pagan marriage. Knowing God makes the difference. When we know God we know that marriage has a higher purpose than to satisfy our lusts or to provide emotional security. Love within the family is holy love, love like God's, love that puts the other person's welfare first. And when we know God we know that persons are important. A woman is not a stove to produce hot food, an electric blanket to keep a man warm, a toy to amuse him when he is bored. She is a person to be treated with full honor and dignity. . . . Faith that works is faith that leads to holiness in the home."[6]

Togetherness. It must not be minimized. Life together is a beautiful venture of faith in which the needs of each other are being fulfilled without an overriding dependency that cripples the other's self-expression. *Togetherness.* Even while apart, thinking of the other and his reaction to what is happening to you, the sense of joyous expectancy at being able to share with him later on. *Togetherness.* Complete trust while apart. Total openness while together. Honesty. No guarding of experiences or withholding for fear of antagonizing or hurting the other.

Such togetherness—mutuality of faith, mutuality of interests—will result in a commitment to each other that no one else can possibly come between. A one-plus-one relationship that is nonmanipulative. It can only deepen love.

THINK ON THESE THINGS

A good marriage is not a contract between just two persons but a sacred covenant between three. Such "threegetherness" requires two people willing not just to live for each other; but two people teaming up earnestly desiring to live for God and each other.

"The Lord will work out his plans for my life—for your lovingkindness, Lord, continues forever" (Ps. 138:8).

15
The Happily Married Do Communicate

"My husband would never have won me if he hadn't done some pretty good talking," said one woman to me. Then she added with a plaintive note, "But he became noncommunicative after marriage."

"I was proud of my wife's conversational ability, she entertained beautifully and we had a good marriage," explained one gentleman. "But somewhere along the line she not only ceased being friendly to others, but the two of us just couldn't communicate."

One marriage counselor was asked, "What is the most essential characteristic of a happy marriage?" He replied, "After love, the ability to confide fully, freely, and frankly in each other."

Another well-known marriage counselor found the failure to converse a "frequent factor in middle-age conflicts and almost universal in all unhappy marriages."

A study in an eastern college determined that nothing is more apt to smooth the course of love than communication; the level of marital satisfaction appeared to be related to the amount of time each day a couple spent talking together. Marriage is really a lifetime of relationships dependent upon communication.[1]

How important it is to communicate even through gestures. Small thoughtful gestures can have a large emotional effect and vastly enrich one's marriage, according to Dr. Carl T. Clarke, a psychology professor at the University of

Florida and director of its Marriage Project. "Less and less we say 'I love you' in words—but positive acts say it, and need to be understood."

Building on positives is a new approach in marriage counseling, according to Norman M. Lobsenz, who researched and wrote an article on the subject for *Christian Herald*.

> When a marriage gets into trouble, many people obsessively focus all their energy and attention on the "problem" causing their difficulties. But often it can be far more saving in such times to concentrate on the positive feelings that brought them together in the first place. Whatever moved them into marriage in the beginning may be more helpful now than any attempt to worry away at the issues that now divide them.[2]

I wonder how many divorces could be prevented if couples would sit down and, instead of firing off a barrage of complaints against each other, would mention the qualities they first admired in each other, the good things they had going for them, the deeper pleasures they shared, the goals they had once mutually set out to reach. This would be positive communication—speaking of each other's virtues and strengths rather than the failings and weaknesses that irritate.

The Bible says there is a time to keep silence and a time to speak. "But where problems exist the deep-freeze of silence is seldom a solution. In marriage, silence like that is dangerous because it shouts that something is wrong. Love can survive large problems better in the open than small ones burning and smouldering within. Silence can make life difficult. Silence is really a lack of love. It implies the other is not worth sharing a concern with, that we don't care what the other thinks, and that the other will not contribute toward an understanding."[3]

What are some common forms of communication-stoppers in marriage? Drescher, in his book *Now Is the Time to Love*, says that words of sarcasm, ridicule, or making fun of the other are forms of hostility that stop the flow of communication. He says that bringing up the past is a good stopper; and urges that if the past must be discussed, then discuss it to completion and forget it. Do it once and for all. Forgive and forget. Making the other person feel cheap or ignorant also stops communication.

Innermost thoughts and feelings must be brought out into the open and shared if marriage is to survive. There is no room for reservation; hearts must be open. A wise philosopher, Erasmus, says that in a truly good marriage, "The wedlock of minds will be greater than that of bodies."[4]

I have to agree, on the basis of my own experience and that of other divorced Christians, that marriages break not always because of talking, but possibly more often because partners do *not* talk. "True communication is self-disclosure, self-revelation without fear. Masks must be dropped. Pretense must be put away. Defenses must fall. Guards must go. Finances, in-laws, sex feelings, child discipline—all these and more must be talked about. It is those couples who feel free to discuss fears and frustrations as well as joys and delights at the deeper levels and without limits, who experience a growing closeness in marriage."[5] Such as these will not be found in divorce courts.

One pastor stated that there was total breakdown in communication before he and his wife were divorced. "I hate to explain it this way," he confided sadly, "but it was hell as far as the conflict in our home was concerned." His explanation was corroborated by the divorced individuals whom I interviewed. The strain that this inflicted upon the children in the home was most pathetic, resulting in a crisis point that had to culminate in divorce for the mental and physical health of everyone involved.

This lack of communication is one important reason why so many men end up spending increasing amounts of time away from home. Men will retreat to hobbies, sports, their work. Many Christian men become immersed in church-related activities, and still others will seek out another woman with whom they can establish some rapport, someone with whom they can communicate.

The same is true for women who will join clubs, the PTA, social work, church meetings, spend more time with their children and their activities. Thus a disproportionate amount of time is given to their mates—anything to avoid a communication confrontation with one's husband. Such women are easy prey for complimentary remarks from other men which can lead to an illicit relationship.

Unless a man or a woman is a complete introvert, or an iceberg type, they simply cannot long endure noncommunication. The greatest tool God gave to us humans to understand each other is communication. If we aren't going to communicate with each other as husbands and wives, you can be certain one or the other, or both, will seek escape routes from the silence barrier that can be more deafening than noise.

Drescher wisely comments:

> Strange, isn't it that a couple falls in love by communication, nourishes it with their unique codes of communication, and unite in the spiritual, emotional, and physical communication of marriage—then suddenly they become speechless! Suddenly they can't or don't get through to each other anymore. . . .
>
> The difference between happiness and unhappiness is not that one marriage has less problems or more problems than another marriage but rather that one couple has learned the art of talking things over and the other has not. Harmony comes and love is strengthened by a frank and honest discussion of differences.[6]

Dr. Gerald Walker Smith, a northern California family therapist, says the best communication occurs when people know where they stand with each other. Strong marriages tend to have the same problem areas as weak ones, but those which succeed apparently do so because the mates are getting through to each other clearly. The happily married do communicate.

Couples should work out a series of domains: his, hers, and mutual. The mutual domain includes sex, child-rearing, mutual friends, in-laws, money, and, to some extent, housekeeping. The main causes of conflict, such as sex, children, and money, are the same in happy and unhappy marriages; but the difference is that happy couples know how to deal with the issues. They've communicated so that they honestly know where they stand. They aren't afraid to level with each other. Fear of one's mate is deadly to success in marriage. It leads to evasion of discussion of issues, withdrawal from one's mate, and outright lying.

Successful communication in marriage takes time. Too many couples who couldn't spend enough time with each other before marriage find themselves drifting apart after marriage. They aren't taking time to discuss the day's activities, to share the little as well as the big things that go into the events of a day. A wife who is cooped up in the house with small children needs time alone with her husband. Husbands and wives who go their separate ways in jobs during the day and come together again at night are often too tired to take the time for a walk, or to read together, or to just sit facing each other making small talk.

As with everything else that requires the use of time, you'll never *find* extra time; you've simply got to *take* it. You've got to make room in your life for those things which are really important. It may mean cutting out some other outside activities or saying no to other people, but a man and a woman need time for each other if communication is to flow. It's worth working at to preserve your marriage.

There is another problem which enters into the matter of communication, and it has to do with understanding of each

169

other. A husband-wife team of lawyer and counselor believe that deep at the root of every marital problem is the simple fact that women rarely understand men, and no man has really ever understood a woman. I recently heard of a book entitled *What Men Know About Women.* The pages of the book are all blank!

"If I could only understand my wife," husbands will complain; and wives will say the same thing regarding their failure to understand their husbands. But in this area, I believe God can give us the understanding we need if we ask him for it. His resources are limitless. He it is who has made us and designed all the intricacies of our emotional makeup. He understands how we function best. And even when we fail at grasping what he would have us to know about our respective mates, then he still holds out patience to us as a virtue we can grasp to aid us in being tolerant and loving even though our understanding at times is limited.

The Apostle Peter wrote, "You husbands must be careful of your wives, being thoughtful of their needs and honoring them as the weaker sex. Remember that you and your wife are partners in receiving God's blessings, and if you don't treat her as you should your prayers will not get ready answers" (1 Pet. 3:7). The fact that the woman is considered weaker does not mean she is to be considered inferior. God made her weaker so that she would depend on her husband, the stronger. A woman is more emotionally vulnerable than a man. Men should recognize this and act accordingly.

Husbands are commanded to love their wives. That is their primary responsibility. When a husband is communicating that love, the woman will respond with love. A man will get from his wife what he invests in her, and that doesn't mean in terms of finances.

The role of a man is to love, lead, protect, and provide for woman. Deprive a man of the sensation of his superior strength and ability to take care of you, and you rob him of his manliness. The age of chivalry is not dead; men still like to be chivalrous. Mental and psychological differences do exist between males and females. Here again, as in other problem areas of marriage, there are books and materials available to help gain an understanding of these differences. It is wise, too, to seek professional help to gain an understanding of one's self. The role of the trained psychologist and counselor is often minimized and even disregarded by some Christians. Many marriages would benefit greatly if the couples would open themselves up honestly to the help that such individuals can give.

Wives are told by the Apostle Peter to "fit in with their husband's plans; for then if they refuse to listen when you talk to them about the Lord, they will be won by your respectful, pure behavior. Your godly lives will speak to them better than any words" (1 Pet. 3:1, 2).

Not all communication in marriage, it can be seen, is through words. Oftentimes our attitudes betray us more than our words. Marriage partners who communicate hear what the other is saying with their minds and their hearts as well as their ears. How beautiful it is to see a couple communicating with their eyes and with touch.

The poet says, "We do not need words. Our eyes speak, our touch reveals. Each new day we discover new beauty in silence, of each other."[7]

A California marriage counselor believes that many marital partners need to be trained in talking and listening to each other. "Many couples do not know how to tackle disagreeable subjects in order to arrive at a reasonable conclusion," says Dr. Harry Adams. "Men in our society have been trained to obedience as children and many avoid fighting at all costs."

Dr. Adams uses the word "fighting" as synonymous with "dealing" and "negotiating." Many passive men will avoid a confrontation simply by walking out the door. For the many divorced people interviewed, I learned that unfortunately this was true—it was true of both partners, though more true with the men. How many couples there are who refuse to talk out their differences and so build up massive walls of unresolved problems and misunderstandings, with barriers that in time become insurmountable, with divorce as the end result. Today, if men and women in marriage are not getting to know each other, it would appear that the most familiar view they are getting of each other is a rapidly retreating figure heading out of the house, slamming the door, running away from facing up to the issues.

Failure to communicate does not necessarily mean absolute silence, according to Dr. A. Dudley Dennison, one of America's leading cardiologists. Dr. Dennison, who is as skillful with words as he is with the scalpel, believes there is that type of communication block which shuts off the deep arterial flow of shared hopes, fears, and dreams. A couple can still go through the superficial routine of "Would you pick up a dozen eggs on the way home from the office?" But the communication block exists, and many such couples are like two strangers sharing a table in a crowded restaurant.

One divorced man told me of his dinner table conversation, which was typical, he said, night after night. Almost without exception they ate their meals in a restaurant.

HE: What kind of a day did you have?
SHE: The usual.
HE: Did you notice how smoggy it was?
SHE: I didn't go outside.
HE: Did we get any mail?
SHE: Bills and second-class mail.
HE: Did you get any phone calls?
SHE: No one bothers to phone me.
HE: Isn't this steak good?
SHE: It's tough.
HE: She's a good little waitress.
SHE: Stop flirting with her.

And on and on and on. Wouldn't that call out the best response in a man? How exciting! What a refined creature she is—so patient, understanding, gentle, kind, and loving. Where was her interest in him? What kind of a day did he have? Did the smog bother him driving on the freeway? Did she say thank you for taking me out for dinner, I really didn't feel like cooking?

More than one divorced individual told me that kind or a similar disgustingly selfish story. There is another side to divorce not discussed in the Bible under the heading of divorce per se. It has to do with communicating our love to our mate through concern about the little things; through encouraging him or her. As women we lose our charm in the eyes of our husbands when we don't smile, when we constantly find fault and nit-pick, when we are sullen, when we cease to be fun to be around. Our words and our attitudes betray us—we are cold and uncaring, thinking only of self. Often, too, our homemaking reflects our selfishness—either we can be too meticulous, or our houses look like pigpens. We want to be treated like queens, but our homes are not our husband's castles; nor do we communicate to him that we think he is our king. Is it any wonder our marriages fall apart?

Dr. Rebecca Liswood, one of the country's foremost marriage counselors, says "those who communicate talk with an objectivity that precludes hostility; and they make certain they have ample opportunity for meaningful talk with their partner."[8]

Television is being blamed as a marriage killer. One blue-ribbon panel of four distinguished authorities in Los Angeles agreed it is the chief reason why the divorce rate is soaring. These experts said TV is a key villain in the tragic American drama we call divorce. They cited 1972 figures that showed that while 2,269,000 couples were being wed, 839,000 marriages were ending in divorce.

Dr. Lawrence Friedman, Los Angeles psychiatrist and

author, summed up the feelings of the panel when he told *The National Enquirer:*

> Thousands of marriages could be saved if husbands and wives would just shut off their TV sets for an hour each night and talk to one another.
>
> Television is more dangerous to our society than the atomic bomb. It's the greatest poison to marriage.
>
> I'm convinced that at least fifty percent of all divorces in the country are unnecessary. And it's all because TV teaches us simple solutions to complex problems. People tell me: "If only I could get rid of this marriage, everything would be all right." Nonsense!
>
> Our teen-agers have grown up watching TV steadily. Because of this, they have everything except the ability to relate to other humans. These "TV orphans" will be the adult divorce statistics of tomorrow.

Another member of the panel, Dr. Paul Popenoe, founder of the American Institute of Family Relations, and a psychologist in Altadena, California, agreed and said:

> Television makes it very easy for husbands and wives to avoid working and talking together to develop their common interests . . . and perhaps save their marriages.
>
> Of course, some marriages should have never taken place. And in these cases, divorce is the only solution.
>
> But I do agree that TV is most definitely a chief reason for disintegration in family life.[9]

What, besides too much TV, is behind this lack of communication between husbands and wives? Why this terrible gulf between a woman and a man who talked before they were married (and chances are, they talked for months afterwards)? It cannot be that there is nothing left to talk about.

Before a couple marry, the man is concerned about pursuing the woman and holding her interest. To do this requires concentrated effort; he knows he can lose her to other interesting suitors and so he puts the proverbial best foot forward. He communicates his love and interest in every possible way.

The woman, on the other hand, is building up her suitor's ego, talking intelligently, expressing an interest in things that interest him, doing all she can so that love will flourish. There is outgoing concern, a giving of herself through thoughtful words and deeds. She would not dream of neglecting him.

But after marriage there is a settling down into the matter of being man and wife. The man has conquered and won; no longer is the conquest on. The woman has, likewise, succeeded in catching her mate. Both begin to let down and relax, often too much so. They begin to take each other for granted. Sometimes it is a simple matter of just forgetting to express affection and appreciation; in other instances, it is sheer neglect; other times there is a definite drawing away from one's partner as discoveries are made about the other that are not quite up to one's expectations. One of the major difficulties can be summed up in the word *selfishness*. We are egocentric.

THINK ON THESE THINGS

You may not be able to understand another's situation; you may not even be able to understand your mate's feelings and reactions to something; but the Bible doesn't say that you have to. The Word of God, however, does admonish us *to be understanding.*

You can communicate understanding by your attitudes and actions as well as words. There is more to communication than words.

"Steer clear of foolish discussions which lead people into the sin of anger with each other. Things will be said that will burn and hurt for a long time to come" (2 Tim. 2:16, 17).

"Don't grumble about each other, brothers. Are you yourselves above criticism? For see! The great Judge is coming. He is almost here. (Let him do whatever criticizing must be done.) (James 5:9).

"Admit your faults to one another and pray for each other so that you may be healed" (James 5:16).

16
First Corinthians 13:
Agape Love

Ten couples celebrating their fiftieth year of living with the same person got together in Los Angeles in the summer of 1973. Said one reporter:

> They were the most married people I had ever seen. There they sat, glowing. . . . They had something. It showed in their eyes. . . . It showed in the way they touched and looked at each other. In the way they walked together out the door to deal with the next fifty years. Whatever it was, it was precious. Whatever it was, it took a long, long time to get.[1]

Love. Who can really define it! One of the golden anniversary celebrants was asked to try. "And what exactly is love, Maggie?"

"It's hard to say," she replied. "But one you've seen it, you won't ever forget it. And once you have it, you pray you'll never lose it."

Walter Trobisch, well-known speaker in Europe, the United States, and Africa on questions of love and marriage, and author of several books on the subject, says very simply:

> Love is a feeling to be learned. It is tension and fulfillment. It is deep longing and hostility. It is gladness and it is pain. There is not one without the other. Happiness is only a part of love—this is what has to be learned.

Suffering belongs to love also. This is the mystery of love, its beauty and its burden. Love is a feeling to be learned.[2]

In a turnabout definition, another writer says love is not giving your wife a pool table for Christmas![3]

It's been said that there are four kinds of people in the world: those in love; those who have been in love; those who are afraid of love; and those who want to love. Where does that find you?

There are countless lonely people walking the face of this earth. "Loneliness is the trip we take when we cannot risk involvement."[4] Many of these lonely people have been hurt by love and loving; and so, they too become statistics. There are at least 36 million American adults, it is believed, who are single—one person for every two and a half who are married. They come in all shapes and sizes, all races and religions, and all temperaments. A great many of these lonely single people are victims of divorce. They have problems that are peculiar to them alone. "With a divorce you come home to four walls," said one very lonely divorced man. "There are great silences you have in your life when you can no longer talk with someone, even though you didn't communicate too well in marriage. Yes, the silences—that's difficult."

"Alone we find solitude, Together we find love," says a sensitive poet.[5]

"A good demanding job is a great solace for loneliness," said another divorced individual. "That goes for a man or a woman," he added. "But I do miss love."

He meant love. Not sex. There is a difference. We talked about that. He missed sex too, but sex is the result of love. Without love, sex is nothing but sex; with love it becomes a unity of two souls. Recently I saw a book dedication which read, "To my wife, the other half of my soul." I would imagine that couple had a great love *and* sex life.

But love is absolutely vital to living. "Without love, you

are nothing, I am nothing, the world is nothing. Love comes first in everything," says the well-known and much-respected Dr. Norman Vincent Peale. "If it were possible to sum up the teachings of Christianity in one word, that word would be love."[6]

No wonder Jesus gathered his disciples around him at their Last Supper together and told them, "I am giving a new commandment to you now—love each other just as much as I love you. Your strong love for each other will prove to the world that you are my disciples" (John 13:34, 35). Jesus made love central to his whole teaching for good reason.

> In its beginning, in its essence, in the simple teachings of Jesus, Christianity is a religion of love. That is basic.
>
> And this emphasis on love is not only for the purpose of making a better world, although a better world will come when we truly love one another. The primary reason for the Gospel stressing love is that a person will actually wither and die ultimately unless he has love in his heart, both for himself and toward other people.[7]

Dr. Peale refers to the great psychiatrist, Smiley Blanton, who wrote a book entitled *Love or Perish*. Either you love or you will perish.

There is so much glib writing and speaking done in regard to love. One hesitates even to try and write on the subject in a book such as this. Where does one begin to try and say something new and meaningful in a book that is dealing with wounded people—individuals who have been so hurt by love and loving. I believe the point of beginning is in that great love chapter in the Bible.

In 1 Corinthians 13 Paul launches into a comprehensive discussion on the nature of love. It is *agape* love that Paul is talking about. You've probably heard many times that the ancient Greeks had three different words for love. Each one was descriptive of a different aspect or level of love.

Briefly, the first word, *eros*, referred to total human love. Eros, from which the English word "erotic" comes, is the kind of love that seeks to get something for one's self. This kind of love may give a little, too, but eros love is not sufficient for a sustaining marital relationship. It is strongly felt that the exaggerated emphasis on eros in our culture is responsible for a large percentage of broken marriages.

Philia is the next higher level of love. It relates to the soul rather than the body. It's the word Peter used when questioned by Christ (John 21:15, 16). A close English word to philia is "friendship." Philia has been described as love's halfway mark—give a little, get a little; a fifty-fifty proposition. "Our" happiness is involved in philia, in contrast to "my" happiness in eros.

Richard L. Strauss makes this observation:

> A couple can make it on this kind of love as long as each one does his part and the circumstances of life remain fairly steady. If one partner fails to contribute his share, however, or if unusual stress is introduced (financial crisis, serious illness, in-law tensions, sexual problems, child-rearing problems, etc.), the friendship suffers. *Philia* can't take the strain. It finally becomes selfish and demanding, and comradeship turns to conflict.[8]

And so we come to *agape* love, God's kind of love. In 1 Corinthians 13 is a description of love rather than a definition. Paul is showing us how agape acts. That couple who aspires to abiding joy in marriage, a marriage that will not end in the divorce court, must have agape.

> Love is very patient and kind, never jealous or envious, never boastful or rude. Love does not demand its own way. It is not irritable or touchy. It does not hold grudges and will hardly notice when others do it wrong. It is never glad about injustice, but rejoices whenever

truth wins out. If you love someone you will be loyal to him no matter what the cost. You will always believe in him, and always stand your ground in defending him . . . love goes on forever (vs. 4–7, with part of vs. 8).

This magnificent discourse on love can revolutionize our homes. But this can only happen when God's Spirit is moving to produce this kind of agape love in our hearts; and *we* have to be willing. God will not force his love upon us, but when we reach out to take what he offers then we are able in our marriage to demonstrate this beautiful selfless love of God himself.

Love, it can be seen from 1 Corinthians 13, is nourished on the milk of human kindness; flourishes on common courtesies that show thoughtfulness; ripens with mutual respect and reverence; and through it all needs constant cultivation.[9]

How do you define love? I believe writer John Drescher is correct when he says that without a doubt love is best defined by what it does.

> When we first fell in love there wasn't anything we weren't willing to do for the one we loved. We would go out of our way to see the other, do anything which we thought might please, and give little gifts to add to the other's joy. Remember that? Somehow we knew love cannot be passive. It is not love until it does something. And interestingly enough, the more we did, the more we loved. Love grows only as it is put into action.[10]

Drescher suggests that marriage partners need to learn all over again the practice of doing nice things for each other, without any reason or fanfare and with no thought of return. The ardor, attention, and thoughtfulness of courtship need to spill over into marriage.

Love will not succumb to an ego bout, either, with an "I

told you so!" attitude. Love is an encouraging sort of thing. Love can be debased by the tint of envy; love can be deteriorated and degraded by the tint of jealousy. Love also has a sense of humor; we must not take ourselves too seriously, for if we do we will be too easily hurt.

Martin Luther exhorted wives to make their husbands glad to come across the threshold at night; and to husbands he said, "Make your wife sorry when you leave."

Fritz Ridenour says, regarding 1 Corinthians 13:

> It almost seems as if sainthood is being asked for in this passage. Not only are you to be a good guy on a white horse; you are supposed to give away the horse and walk through the desert yourself. It helps, however, if you slice 1 Corinthians 13 about three ways: verses 1–4 tell you to be real; verses 5–7 tell you to put others first; and verses 8–13 tell you to "be in touch"—that is, with God.[11]

Love produces love; to insist on our own rights and strike back at our marriage partner even when he is unlovable will only prolong the conflict, whatever it may be. We are to keep on expressing the patient love of God, and the promise is, ultimately, it will bring us genuine love in return. I think the old country parson had something when he said, "Love, like a spring rain, is pretty hard to be in the middle of without getting some on you."

Love requires acceptance, patience, and understanding; we might say time, warmth, and care. "Love is an attitude . . . in constant motion as the sea."[12]

It is said that the matter of violated rights is probably one of the most common troublespots in shaky marriages. Here is where 1 Cor. 13:5 love—"Love seeks not her own"—comes into focus. True biblical meekness says to give up your own rights for that one you love. The key to doing this lies in complete yieldedness of self, first of all to God. If he has our all, then we can honestly and happily surrender ourselves to our marriage partner.

Love isn't going to wear its feeling on its sleeve. The touchy you needs the touch of God for victory.

If you are magnifying the faults of your mate, you are a likely candidate for the divorce mill. If you are tabulating all the weaknesses of your partner, dwelling on his or her shortcomings, and continually dragging up past grievances, then you are not loving your husband or wife. You are not to take into account a wrong suffered (vs. 5b).

One major contributing factor to failure in marriage comes when one or the other broadcasts the faults of their mate. "Love is to bear all things" verse 7; love is to endure all things, verse 7b. True love will keep confidential those things that are no one else's business. If your wife has been unfaithful to you, and it is your desire to keep your marriage together, and you really feel you love her, then it is your duty as a loving husband to keep quiet about it to others. You cannot expect to regain her love by letting the world know she has failed you. The same goes for a wife whose husband has stepped out of bounds. True love is protective, defending the other, magnifying the other's good points. If you really love your mate and want to keep your marriage together, then you will practice what this verse in 1 Corinthians 13 says. I didn't say it, but the Bible does.

True love will not put its mate through the third degree constantly. "Even when he's been guilty of adultery?" the heartbroken wife asks. "How can I trust him?" That is the decision—either you decide to trust him, or you may as well face the fact that your love is not what it's supposed to be. You surely will not win back his love by disbelieving him every time he comes in the door ten minutes late. Maybe he really did get tied up in freeway traffic. Love keeps on believing, verse 7. Real love will weather every assault.

Love is also willing to take responsibility; love is giving, not seeing what you can get out of it. Love will not exploit its mate. Love thinks more of its wife or husband than it does of itself.

Love like this never fails; it is a permanent and perpetual grace, lasting into eternity. "It never falls to pieces, never collapses, never terminates. As long as the Spirit of God is in control of our lives He just keeps on producing love and we just keep on displaying it!"[13]

There are some of us who have failed in the love department with our mates. Ours was not agape 1 Corinthians 13 love, to begin with, or it would have survived. This does not mean we are not capable of such agape-type loving. The word love has been called the most beautiful word in the English language. That love was demonstrated supremely in the love God had for us, while we were yet sinners, in sending Christ to die for us (Rom. 5:8).

Words are very limiting—even for writers, who are supposed to be the most prolific with them. But when it comes to expressing one's feelings about love, even we must confess to great inadequacy. I can only leave you in this chapter with the love of God; his love never gives up. As divorced individuals, some of us did give up; but thank God he doesn't give up on us.

Think on These Things

Self-love of the possessive, self-centered variety shackles the hearts and spirits and minds of those we "love." Are you tying someone in knots because you love yourself wrongly? If so, you are not only binding that person, you are binding yourself as well. And your *self* is meant to be free.

"If the Son shall make you free, you shall be free indeed." Jesus meant this for everyone. This is why he longs for us to love ourselves enough, and in the right way, so we will want to be free.

If you aren't, first of all, concerned for the welfare and freedom of the person you think you love, then you are mistaken in your idea of real love. If you are constantly being hurt and slighted by someone, it isn't because you love that person so much. It is because you love *you* in a self-protecting, egocentric way. You will suffer, if this is true, but perhaps not as much as those who really love you and hate the destructiveness of your misplaced self-love.

To love ourselves rightly, we must leave ourselves free to be whole persons in the midst of anything life can hand us. When we love and respect ourselves this way, we will have tapped the Source of love, and will find ourselves able to give constructive, creative devotion to those whom God has given us to love.

To love ourselves rightly, we must love ourselves *in God*.[14]

Love Christians everywhere (1 Pet. 2:17).

17
Divorce Is . . .

Divorce is not a solution; it is not *the* answer that automatically insures that the one seeking the divorce is going to live happily ever after. We carry ourselves with us out of divorce; and often, we are our own worst problem.

Divorce is not easy. It is tough and unpleasant. It is difficult to discuss; and even more difficult for me to write about.

Divorce is hurtful. Hurtful to many people—not just the ones involved in the divorce action. Hurtful to the cause of Christ.

Divorce is ugly. Ugly to onlookers, ugly to those who can only surmise the whys and wherefores. Ugly to children. Ugly to those affected the most—the man and the woman.

Divorce is costly. Financially. Emotionally. Physically. Spiritually. A couple may have worked and sacrificed years to attain a measure of financial security, to have built up an equity in a home, to have acquired some bonds and something to provide for their future, only to have much of this wiped out through costly lawyer and court costs. Divorce plays havoc with one's emotions and health. The marital situation can and often does do this also, but the actual divorce doesn't help one's ulcers, tension headaches, colitis, nerves, and whatever it is that may be draining one physically. And unless one is very careful, divorce and the attendant stigma, alienation, and fears about what others may think or say can throw you into a tailspin spiritually.

Divorce is painful. It is a chaotic time. A time of sadness, struggle, anguish, anxiety, and trauma. Count on it, you will shed some tears if you are at all sensitive—and this includes men as well as women.

But sometimes divorce is necessary. Necessary for survival. Necessary to retain one's sanity and sense of personal worth. Necessary for one's physical health and emotional stability.

Sometimes divorce is the lesser of two evils—the evil of living in a marriage that is subideal and a pretense, a lie causing you to live as a hypocrite, maintaining a false front, a facade of happiness when inside there is nothing but unhappiness, unpeace, and turmoil.

Divorce does not mean that you have to live as a remnant from a personal disaster. Many divorced individuals with whom I talked confessed that they regarded their divorce action as a door to a new life. They did not regard it as such, necessarily, at the time they were going through the divorce; but time does heal even the wounds caused by divorce. Most of the people were willing to admit that the divorce jarred them into reappraising themselves. They had to come to grips with themselves, and while the revelation was startling and not altogether pleasant, it did offer insight into their emotions and personality. With the help of psychotherapy and spiritual counseling and the love of Christian friends and family members, they did survive and are better individuals for it today.

One woman made this confession:

> It was a devastating blow to my ego. My pride took a terrific wallop, and it really did send me reeling. But hindsight is better than no sight, and now I can objectively sit back and tell you that I really was a witch in my marriage.
>
> I know I'm a much better woman today and I'll not

make those same mistakes in a second marriage. I'm sure I sent my husband into the arms of other women—I think he did have a problem, he was his own worst enemy in this regard—but I might have been able to prevent this with the understanding I now have of myself.

Divorce is a tragedy; but it can help us face the future if we honestly try to understand the past and stop trying to justify our actions, blaming our former mates.

Divorce can bring us to the point where we appraise our values and set new goals. Where marriage partners have been destroying one another for years with their uncontrolled tongues, now the opportunity presents itself to rebuild one's shattered ego, to regain one's dignity and feeling of self-worth. It takes time, but the growth of personality does not need to stop. One can become productive and creative. New friends can be made, new interests cultivated.

Divorced persons of both sexes owe it to themselves and their children to come out of the experience as unharmed as possible. The negative reaction of the Christian world to divorce does not have to throw the divorced Christian into a state of despair. Stop blaming yourself. And don't panic. It's a big world out there, but there is a place for you in it. A worthy place, an enjoyable place. A place for you to share your faith and the goodness and greatness of God. If you have experienced his mercy and love, think now in terms of the meaningful way you can let this be known from the depths of your own personal experience.

Divorce can serve as a teacher. There are some lessons in life we'd just as soon forget; divorce can help us do that as we learn new lessons. We can make the divorce work for us, reshaping our thinking, redefining our values. Divorce can help us mature—too many of us act like spoiled children in our marriages, insisting on having our own way, neurotic, whining, complaining. Selfish. There is nothing like a divorce to snap you to attention when there is no one there to cater to your every whim.

Divorce can develop your inner strengths as you look away from people and things and place your reliance on God's strength and support. It is important that an individual have a proper self-image; the Bible says we are to love our neighbor as we love ourselves (Lev. 19:18). When there is recognition that you are important to the Lord and loved by him, you begin to see the need to shape up if you are to be of service to him. You must believe in yourself—yes, have the right kind of self-love and believe the fact that in choosing divorce you have not made the unforgivable mistake. As you learn to face reality, your true potential has a chance to develop as you reach out to accept new challenges. If you have made a genuine attempt through the years to save your marriage, you need not carry a burden of guilt nor feel you have to make excuses and apologies. The divorced individual does not have to reap a harvest of despair.

THINK ON THESE THINGS

Regarding Christian behavior to one another the Apostle Paul said:

> We who have strong faith ought to shoulder the burden of the doubts and qualms of others and not just to go our own sweet way. Our actions should mean the good of others—should help them to build up their characters. For even Christ did not choose his own pleasure, but as it is written:
>
> > The reproaches of them that reproached
> > thee fell upon me.

For all those words which were written long ago are meant to teach us today; that when we read in the scriptures of the endurance of men and of all the help that God gave them in those days, we may be encouraged to go on hoping in our own time. May the God who inspires men to endure, and gives them a Father's care, give you a mind united toward one another because of your common loyalty to Jesus Christ. And then, as one man, you will sing from the heart the praises of God the Father of our Lord Jesus Christ. So open your hearts to one another as Christ has opened his heart to you, and God will be glorified (Rom. 15:1–7, *PT*).

18
Is Divorce Unpardonable?

Recently I read the statement of an athlete who said it was great to come home to his dog. "My dog doesn't care whether I win or lose," he commented. Dogs are great company. I speak from the experience of having a German shepherd who nuzzled her way into my heart in a touching way. But for all her loving ways, Christy couldn't kiss away my tears. Christy was fun to play with, especially when I threw the Frisbee to her and we romped in the back yard; but Christy couldn't laugh with me or do other fun things that require another person. Christy was good protection in the darkness and lonely hours of night—there were many nights when I'm certain her barking and growls kept intruders away—but Christy couldn't put her arms around me and whisper, "Don't be afraid." Neither could Christy say to me, "I love you. I accept you just as you are—faults and all; no one is perfect you know."

And I love books too. Books are marvelous company; and writing them is wonderful and rewarding, even though it requires tremendous discipline and a great amount of hard work. When the books are written and published, when they stand there on my shelf, I can take them down, open them, hold them in my hands, and sit down and reread what has been written; but those books can't ease away my hurting and hungering for the companionship of someone to love. Those books can't hold my hands, or tell me I look great, or that I look tired and should take it easy. I can't walk into church with my dog and the books I've written and join in worship with other couples. I can't go to the home of friends or to a party with my books tucked under my arm and Christy on a leash and expect to feel welcome or have a good time. I might cook a beautiful roast beef dinner with all the trimmings and offer it to Christy—she'd snatch it up fast enough—but when she'd devoured it all, she'd only sit there wagging her tail. She couldn't say, "You're a great cook—just another thing I love about you!"

What I am saying I say for all divorced Christians who need love, understanding and companionship. And should they remarry, they need acceptance.

I have now remarried. Several of the people whom I interviewed and who shared with me much of what has been written in this book have also now remarried. The will of the Lord has been sought and there is peace, happiness, and love.

In the process of working on the final revision of this book I took time out for an autographing at a local bookstore (for another book that had just been released). A woman who knew me, knew of the divorce and my remarriage, came into the store and, in the presence of the bookstore manager and his wife and others, proceeded to point an accusing finger at me, questioning whether we had done the right thing, did we know the joy of the Lord, were we living at peace with God, how did we reconcile remarriage with God's Word, did I honestly think God would bless our marriage and that it would last, and so on.

Contrast that kind of attitude and behavior with that of another Christian friend who wrote a letter of recommendation for my husband in which he stated (among other kind and helpful things):

As a dispassionate observer, his [my husband's] previous marriage was one of those tragedies which come upon people even though they do all they can to salvage the relationship. Over the years, he patiently and with long suffering tried to rectify the situation. From my own personal knowledge and the views of others, I've concluded that he was caught in an impossible situation, of which he had only one option in order to recover a strong ego-identification as a person and male and to be able to continue to be self-fufilling and useful in the Lord's service.

This same friend has offered that kind of love and understanding to both our former mates. He exemplifies the kind of forgiving love in action which Christ gave as the example.

There are some individuals for whom marriage to begin with was wrong; they can function better in a single state. There are others who make wrong, immature choices, not seeking the mind of the Lord. There are many divorced people who will never feel the need and desire to remarry; they can be content just as they now are. Others of us, however, are not at our best in an alone single state; the pieces of our lives fit better, we are fulfilled persons, now that we have finally met someone with whom we feel a depth of love and understanding we did not have before. We are now better able to do the Lord's work, to identify with others, to be more productive.

While I was shaken and deeply hurt—yes, I *am* human—by what the woman said to me and tried to do in the bookstore as I sat autographing copies of my book entitled *Forgiveness in Action*, yet God put words in my mouth to silence her accusations and insinuations. I was able to say to her, "I love you in the Lord, but you do make it very difficult." For you see, dear reader, there can be peace, there is the joy of the Lord, there is hope, love, and a new life for divorced people. Divorce is not the unforgivable sin. God is merciful.

How thankful I am for God's Word—his Word is so precious. He is a God who is near. He is not far off from divorced people who call upon him, seeking his forgiveness, acknowledging their sinfulness, pleading Christ's blood. To Isaiah the prophet God gave the assurance that he would guard and support him. That same guidance and support are for the divorced Christian, and for the divorced remarried Christian.

> But now the Lord who created you says, "Don't be afraid, for I have ransomed you; I have called you by name; you are mine. When you go through deep waters and great trouble, I will be with you. When you go down through rivers of difficulty, you will not drown! When you walk through the fire of oppression, you will not be burned up—the flames will not consume you. For I am the Lord God, your Savior . . . you are precious to me and honored, and I love you" (Isa. 43:2-4).

I dare to believe that God is going to answer the prayers that covered the writing of this book, difficult as it has been.

Can marriages be put back together? Yes!

Can broken lives be salvaged and restored? Yes!

Can children of divorce be helped? Yes!

Can young people embarking upon the sea of matrimony read and learn? Can young people searching for a life partner find direction? Yes!

And can divorced people themselves receive help, and is there hope for them? Yes!

And can divorced remarried people begin life anew? Yes!

Yes, *with God*, through Christ and the power of the Holy Spirit operating in their lives.

Yes, if you, the reader, will give them a chance—if you, by the grace of God, will exhibit his mercy, forgiveness, understanding, and love.

Bibliographical Notes

CHAPTER 2

1. Helen B. Andelin, *Fascinating Womanhood* (Santa Barbara, Calif.: Pacific Press, 1963).

CHAPTER 3

1. A. Berkeley Mickelsen, "Biblical Perspectives on Marriage and Divorce," *Standard*, February 23, 1970, p. 17.
2. Leighton Ford, "Is the Family Doomed?" *Sacramento Reachout*, May 21, 1973, reprinted from *Crusade Information Service*, Leighton Ford Crusade.
3. Mickelsen.
4. Ibid.

CHAPTER 5

1. *Los Angeles Times*, April 20, 1971.
2. Mel Krantzler, *Creative Divorce* (New York: M. Evans & Co., 1973), pp. 28, 31. Reprinted by permission of the publishers, M. Evans & Co., Inc., New York, N.Y. 10017.
3. Ibid., p. 99.

CHAPTER 6

1. Jean Murphy, "Panel on Divorce Stresses Need for Marital Counseling," *Los Angeles Times*, April 20, 1971.
2. Ibid.
3. Lars Granberg, "Divorce and Remarriage," *Baker's Dictionary of Practical Theology*, ed. Ralph G. Turnbull (Grand Rapids: Baker Book House, 1967), pp. 221–24.
4. James Montgomery Boice, "The Biblical View of Divorce," *Eternity*, December, 1970, p. 19.
5. K. C. Pillai, *Light through an Eastern Window* (New York: Robert Speller & Sons, 1967), p. 1.
6. Jack MacArthur, *Marriage and Divorce* (Burbank, Calif.: Voice of Calvary), p. 8.

CHAPTER 8

1. William Touhy, "Divorce in Italy—Many Still Fear Its Stigma," *Los Angeles Times*, February 11, 1972.
2. Ibid.
3. Bernard L. Ramm, *The Right, the Good and the Happy* (Waco, Tex.: Word Books, 1971), p. 88.
4. Touhy.
5. Drew J. Gunnells, Jr., "Divorce American Style," *The Cutting Edge: Critical Questions for Contemporary Christians*, vol. 2, compiled by H. C. Brown, Jr. (Waco, Tex.: Word Books, 1969), p. 51.
6. Ramm, p. 88.
7. James L. Johnson, "Divorced Persons: Do They Have a Place in Your Church?" *Christian Life*, Wheaton, Ill., May, 1970.
8. Gunnells, p. 51.
9. A. Berkeley Mickelsen, "Biblical Perspectives on Marriage and Divorce," *Standard*, February 23, 1970, p. 19.
10. Thomas Cosgrove, "What Divorced Catholics Need Most," *Liguorian*, March, 1973, pp. 30, 31.
11. Catharine Brandt, "Facing Divorce," *Success*, Baptist Pub., Denver, Colo., Spring, 1971.
12. Ibid.
13. R. Lofton Hudson, *Helping Each Other Be Human* (Waco, Tex.: Word Books, 1970).
14. David R. Mace, "The Pastor and Divorce," *Pastoral Psychology*, September, 1968, p. 65.
15. Faris D. Whitesell, "The Pastor Faces the Divorce Problem," *Gospel Herald and Sunday School Times*, September 1, 1970.
16. Gunnells, p. 51.

CHAPTER 9

1. Bernard L. Ramm, *The Right, the Good and the Happy*, (Waco, Tex.: Word Books, 1971), p. 88.
2. J. Louise Despert, *Children of Divorce* (New York: Doubleday).
3. Ramm, p. 84.
4. Carol Mindey, *The Divorced Mother* (New York: McGraw-Hill, 1969), p. 95.
5. Jack Waugh, "Amateur Parents, Professional Kids—Children:Deeply Affected by a Broken Home," *Christian Science Monitor*, June 23, 1971.
6. Richard A. Gardner, *The Boys and Girls Book About Divorce* (New York: Science House, 1970).
7. Ibid.
8. Ibid.

9. Ibid.
10. Newton Frohlich, *Making the Best of It—A Guide to Negotiating a Divorce* (New York: Harper & Row, 1971).
11. Mindey, p. 7.
12. Ibid., p. 8.
13. Ibid., p. 8.

CHAPTER 11

1. "Higher Divorce Rate Hits Older Marriages," *Los Angeles Times*, July 5, 1973.
2. Faris D. Whitesell, "The Pastor Faces the Divorce Problem," *Gospel Herald and Sunday School Times*, September 1, 1970.
3. Ibid.

CHAPTER 12

1. C. S. Lovett, *Divorce Problem* (Baldwin Park, Calif.: Personal Christianity, 1959, 1964), p. 25.
2. Ibid., pp. 74, 75.
3. Ibid., pp. 21,22.
4. Ibid., p. 29.
5. Ibid., p. 72.

CHAPTER 13

1. Tim LaHaye, *How to Be Happy Though Married* (Wheaton, Ill.: Tyndale House, 1968).

CHAPTER 14

1. Jack Waugh, "War in the Living Room: The Assault of Change," *Christian Science Monitor*, June 22, 1971.
2. Gilliam Franks, "The Man You Married—Do You Really Know Him?" *Santa Ana Register*, June 1, 1971.
3. David Augsburger, *How Does Your Marriage Add Up?* (Harrisonburg, Va.: The Mennonite Hour, 1967).
4. Billy Graham, "My Answer," *Fullerton Daily News Tribune*, March 17, 1973.
5. Henry Wildeboer, "The Minister's Workshop: Rebuilding Marital Fidelity," *Christianity Today*, June 18, 1971.
6. David A. Hubbard, "Faith That Works," *Today's Christian*, October, 1972, pp. 1, 6.

CHAPTER 15

1. John M. Drescher, *Now Is the Time to Love* (Scottdale, Pa.: Herald Press, 1970) p. 40.

2. Norman M. Lobsenz, "Marriage Is an Edifice That Must Be Rebuilt Every Day," *Christian Herald*, April, 1972, p. 59.
3. Drescher, p. 41.
4. Drescher, pp. 44, 45.
5. Drescher, p. 45.
6. Drescher, pp. 38, 39.
7. Walter Rinder, *Love Is an Attitude* (Millbrae, Calif.: Celestial Arts, 1970).
8. Rebecca Liswood, M.D., with Adele Whitley Fletcher, "Say No to Divorce," *Lady's Circle*, April, 1973.
9. Alan Markfield, "4 Leading Experts on Marriage Blame Television for Soaring Divorce Rate," *National Enquirer*, April 8, 1973.

CHAPTER 16
1. Jim Stingley, "Fifty Years—For Better or for Worse," *Los Angeles Times*, July 8, 1973.
2. Walter Trobisch, *Love Is a Feeling to Be Learned* (Baden-Baden, Germany: Editions Trobisch, 1971. Used by permission of Inter Varsity Press, Downers Grove, Ill.).
3. Jon Beull, "Love Is Not Giving Your Wife a Pool Table for Christmas," *Collegiate Challenge*, October, 1971.
4. George Betts, *My Gift to You* (Millbrae, Calif.: Celestial Arts Publishing, 1970).
5. Walter Rinder, *Love Is an Attitude*, (Millbrae, Calif.: Celestial Arts Publishing, 1970).
6. Norman Vincent Peale, *Loves Comes First in Creative Living* (Foundation for Christian Living, May, 1972).
7. Ibid.
8. Richard L. Strauss, *Marriage Is for Love* (Wheaton, Ill.: Tyndale House, 1973), pp. 41, 42.
9. John M. Drescher, *Now Is the Time to Love* (Scottdale, Pa.: Herald Press, 1970), p. 28.
10. Ibid., p. 28.
11. Fritz Ridenour, *I'm a Good Man, But . . .* (Glendale, Calif.: G/L Publications, 1969), p. 68.
12. Rinder.
13. Strauss, p. 51.
14. Eugenia Price, *A Woman's Choice* (Grand Rapids: Zondervan Publishing House, 1962).